MODE OF PRODUCTION
AND SOCIAL FORMATION

By the same authors
PRE-CAPITALIST MODES OF PRODUCTION

Also by Barry Hindess
THE DECLINE OF WORKING CLASS POLITICS
THE USE OF OFFICIAL STATISTICS IN SOCIOLOGY
PHILOSOPHY AND METHODOLOGY IN THE SOCIAL
    SCIENCES
SOCIOLOGICAL THEORIES OF THE ECONOMY (*editor*)

Also by Paul Hirst
DURKHEIM, BERNARD AND EPISTEMOLOGY
SOCIAL EVOLUTION AND SOCIAL CATEGORIES

MODE OF PRODUCTION AND SOCIAL FORMATION

An Auto-Critique of *Pre-Capitalist Modes of Production*

BARRY HINDESS and PAUL HIRST

First edition 1977
Reprinted 1978

Published by
THE MACMILLAN PRESS LTD
London and Basingstoke
Associated companies in Delhi
Dublin Hong Kong Johannesburg Lagos
Melbourne New York Singapore Tokyo

ISBN 0 333 22344 6 (hardcover)
ISBN 0 333 22345 4 (paperback)

Typeset by
Pioneer (Graphics)
Printed in Great Britain by
Unwin Brothers Limited
Woking and London

Contents

Acknowledgements

We should like to thank Stephen Savage, who made an important contribution to the critique of epistemology advanced here, as well as providing useful criticisms of the manuscript, and also Roland Anrup for numerous pertinent questions and critical points.

B. H.
P. H.

Introduction

This text is the product of another, *Pre-Capitalist Modes of Production* (hereafter *PCMP*). It is a critique of and a continuation of our earlier work. A critique: certain of the central concepts and problems in *PCMP* are rejected in this text. A continuation: this rejection is possible only because of the very concepts and problems produced in *PCMP*. The form of criticism practised here is not a simple rejection, rather it is a working on the unevennesses of the earlier text, it is a means of and a part of new theoretical work. This introduction will review the principal unevennesses at issue and outline our response to them.

Both of the main areas of unevenness in *PCMP* are a function of its relation in turn to an earlier text, to *Reading Capital*. *PCMP* may be regarded as a radical, but by no means complete, break from the work of Althusser and Balibar. Although we rejected Balibar's project of a *general* theory of modes of production, we remained committed to the possibility of constructing concepts of modes of production. We criticised *Reading Capital'*s conception of modes as social totalities determined 'in the last instance' by the economic, and generating, as 'structures in dominance', the ideological and political structures and effects necessary to their existence and reproduction as totalities. Instead, *PCMP* conceived modes as concepts of an economic structure and of the conditions necessary for its existence, but it insisted that these conditions and their effects could not be given in or derived from the concept of the economy. Mode of production was not a self-conditioning social whole; it could not, therefore, function as Balibar's concepts did as the elements of a theory of history. In *PCMP* the concepts of pre-capitalist modes were formed as part of a process of theoretical work, as a solution to theoretical problems which would make it possible to produce concepts relevant to the current situation.

The present text rejects the pertinence of the concept of mode of production. The effect of concentration on the conceptualisation of modes of production is the restriction of analysis to an extremely limited range of economic class relations and the consequent neglect of the problems of conceptualising more complex forms of class relations. We argue that it is necessary to develop concepts of economic class relations and their conditions of existence in definite social formations.

The classic concept of mode of production, developed by Marx and retained in substance by Althusser, is that of a definite form of social *totality*, a form capable of historical existence as a society. The concept appropriates this concrete reality/possibility in thought: the nature and limits of the concept are the nature and limits of the being of the object. The object exists as it is conceived in the order of knowledge. *PCMP* denied the possibility of the operation denoted by this concept of the 'appropriation of the concrete in thought' (a concept Althusser adopted and developed from Marx's usage in his 1857 Introduction to *A Contribution to the Critique of Political Economy*). It denied in consequence not only that the concrete could be *known* in this way, but that it existed in this *way*. The notion of appropriation (of the concrete in the abstract) supposed its object existed in the form of its knowledge. The denial of the form of knowledge necessarily denied the objects or entities constituted by it: that is, self-conditioning social totalities whose determinations and effects could be apprehended in abstraction as generalities. The form of causality corresponding to such entities (totalities-generalities) is one of effects which are necessary in the concept; such effects specified in the general concept are, at best, modified or counteracted in the concrete conditions of their application. This is necessarily so, the concrete must be apprehended in its determinations if it is 'appropriated' in thought, and these determinations must (in essence) be general if they are capable of expression in abstraction. In denying this form of causality we denied the possibility of its effects; rejecting causes-as-generalities meant rejecting general concrete effects of concepts. It meant rejecting any general and necessary form of the historical process, whether it be the evolution and supersession or the self-reproduction of a mode of production. The form in which a historical process is conceived is a product of the type of causality assigned to the social totalities which generate and support it. *PCMP* in denying knowledge as the abstraction of the essence of the concrete (complete with its determinations) denied the possibility of any philosophy of history.

In *PCMP* these denials in practice took the form of insisting that the conditions of existence of social relations could not be given in the concepts of those relations (denial of auto-existence) and that social effectivity existed in the results of the balance of forces in the class struggle (these results forming the conditions of new balances). Thus social explanation always required theorisation of the 'current situation' and general concepts merely served as means of analysis of these situations. General concepts provided categories of the *relations* of the class struggle and not its effects. These concepts were not essentially prior explanations of these struggles, reducing them to products of a causality already given in the concept.

This break from *Reading Capital* was partial and not unproblematic. The conditions of existence of economic relations were not provided by the action of these relations themselves. However, in *PCMP* the structure of the *economic* was conceived in a way which resembled the conception of the *social totality* in *Reading Capital.* The thesis of the necessary and general dominance of the relations over the forces of production is the locus of this problem. It reveals the effect of not displacing completely the classical concept of mode of production and the forms of causality associated with it. *The forces of production were derived from the concept of the relations.* This derivation was conceived as a necessary and general concrete effect. It was argued in the text that this effect reflected the primacy of the class struggle. Here one encounters a systematic conflation of the order of discourse (derivation of the concept of the forces from the concept of the relations) with the order of causality (this discursive order mirrors the causal order of the real). This conflation can only be defended on the basis of the notion of 'appropriation' which we had rejected. This general dominance of the relations of production is exactly like the concept of the 'determination by the economic in the last instance'. (It should be noted that this criticism extends only to the general concept of the forces/relations connection; the specific working-out of the concepts in particular chapters often produces results which differ from or are not reducible to this, for example Chapter 5.)

This general dominance is problematic not merely on general theoretical grounds. The nature of the means of production to be possessed will affect the forms of their possession, and the forms of organisation of production will affect the distribution between possessors and non-possessors. Certain means of and forms of organisation of production form conditions of existence of relations of production. Are these conditions necessarily given by the relations as specified in their concept? Clearly, definite social formations can impose certain conditions of the forces which affect the form of the relations. Once mode of production is conceived not as a social totality but as a concept of the economic level, then its very nature as a necessary combination of forces and relations of production becomes untenable.

The form of defence of the primacy of the relations of production in *PCMP* is to insist on the primacy of the class struggle. Technique, and therefore the forces, once given dominance, negate this determinant role. This negative argument is hardly a defence for the dominance of the relations. This appeal to the class struggle is an attempt to provide an ontological privilege (for the relations as the origin of that struggle) which will support this discursive privilege of the relations. It corresponds to attempts to ground the primacy of the economic, to insist on its 'materiality' and on the materialist thesis of the primacy of the means of subsistence. It is the general discursive privilege assigned to the concepts which requires this privileged ontological status for the entities specified in these concepts. These privileged statuses (the product of the conflation of the orders of discourse and causality) can be challenged. In the case of the relations of production:

whilst the relations of production define the classes, do not all levels of the social formation, including the forces of production, provide conditions of existence for and arenas of the class struggle? The relations are not a privileged locus of this struggle or its effects. In the case of the economic level: how can the simple necessity of men providing their means of subsistence explain the diversity and complexity of the forms in which it is provided? The effectivity of the forces cannot be derived from the concept of the relations. Indeed, and this is a major point made in *PCMP* (but subverted by the general dominance of the relations), 'forces' and 'relations' cannot be conceived as separate *things,* linked externally by a causal effect. In the concepts of definite social formations the forms of distribution of the means of production are combined with definite means and forms of production organisation. This combination affects the form of the relations: both of these categories must be understood as providing means of conceptualising forms which condition one another and yet are combined as a single structure of social relations.

We have no doubt that we shall be told by the unreconstructed defenders of 'orthodoxy' that to abandon the determination of the economic (in either the first or last instances) is to abandon Marxism. That may be. But Marxism has been abandoning 'orthodoxy' since the 1850s. Marx and Engels, with varying success, and virtually every other major Marxist thinker (Gramsci and Althusser being the most systematic in their opposed ways) have been in retreat from the consequences of economism. Where these consequences have not been abandoned in political practice (as they generally are in the case of Lenin or Mao), the results have generally been disastrous.

There is no general priority to the economic over other levels of the social formation, or of the relations over the forces. However, we would argue that it is important to give the concepts of the relations *priority in discourse,* that is, in the method of working to begin the formation of concepts of definite social formations with concepts of relations and the problems posed by them and then proceed to a specification of the other forms upon which these relations are conditional. The effect of this specification will be to modify the concepts which formed the point of departure. Discursive priority does not make the concepts in question a privileged level from which all others are derived.

However that may be, it is clear that the conception of the articulated combination of forces and relations of production adopted in *PCMP* (a conception which modifies but retains the positions of *Reading Capital*) must be rejected. Rejecting this conception is to reject the theoretical basis of the unity of the concept of mode of production (it *is* this combination). It follows that the elements of this articulated combination once separated need to be reconceptualised. In the final chapter of this book we discuss the concept of the relations of production anew, posing it in relation to the possession and separation of the means of production. We argue that it is necessary to develop (instead of concepts of modes of production) concepts of relations of production and their conditions of existence, further specifying these concepts by developing the forms in which these conditions are provided in definite social formations. As the concept of mode of production is displaced, so the concepts of relations of production and social formations gain in theoretical importance.

The arguments outlined above are possible because of the rejection of the notion of the 'appropriation of the concrete in thought'. This position was explicitly taken in *PCMP* but its consequences were far from clearly worked through in that text. Our conception of the nature and status of theoretical work represented an attempt to break from Althusserian rationalism without at the same time retreating into empiricism. It could hardly be said that the epistemological reflections in *PCMP* are consistent or entirely successful in attaining these objectives. Subsequent to *PCMP* we were led to reformulate our position, not in terms of a new account of the relation of 'knowledge' to the 'concrete', but by means of a rejection of epistemological discourse itself. This critique of epistemology enabled us to clarify and to develop the implications of our rejection of rationalist and empiricist epistemological doctrines. We must insist, confident

that we shall be misread, that our rejection of the
epistemological category of 'concrete' is not an idealist
denial of the significance or reality of (material) objects.
That denial is a position within epistemology which
substitutes other (spiritual) objects as appropriate to
knowledge. We do not deny the *existence* of social relations -
that would render our very project absurd. What we reject
is the *category* of 'concrete' as object-of-knowledge. It is the
relation of 'appropriation' or of 'correspondence' of
knowledge to its objects which we challenge. In the first
chapter of this text we outline our critique of epistemology.
In the third chapter we examine the relation of Marxist
theoretical work and political practice to social relations.
This is a relation which rejects the category of 'knowledge',
the notion of an 'object' of knowledge (a form of being
corresponding to the form in which it must be known - its
form differing in rationalist or empiricist epistemologies),
and also general epistemological criteria of validity of
knowledge (which specify validity in terms of criteria for
determining correspondence or appropriation).

One final point of substance is necessary in this
introduction. Throughout this text we refer to theory as
theoretical *discourse*. Why do we use this term? Theoretical
discourse we shall define as the construction of problems for
analysis and solutions to them by means of concepts.
Concepts are deployed in ordered successions to produce
these effects. This order is the order created *by the practice
of theoretical work itself*: it is guaranteed by no necessary
'logic' or 'dialectic' nor by any necessary mechanism of
correspondence with the real itself. Theoretical work
proceeds by constant problematisations and reconstructions.
Theories only exist as *discourses* - as concepts in definite
orders of succession producing definite effects (posing,
criticising, solving problems) - as a result of that order.
Theoretical discourse, like discourse in general, speaking and
writing, is an unlimited process. Classically, in epistemologies,
theories have an appropriate form of order in which their
relation to the real is revealed. They appropriate, correspond
to or are falsified by the real. The limits of nature set their
limits. Theory ultimately represents and is limited by the

order of the real itself. In empiricist epistemologies, for
example, theories take the form of categories translatable
into definite observation statements. Our conception of
discourse cannot be so limited. This is not to deny 'reality'
exists, is ordered, or to assert that it is infinite and
unknowable - all of these are sceptical or critical positions
within epistemological discourse. We reject the category of
reality-in-general as epistemological; it is the couple of
knowledge-in-general. Thus we would argue that it is necessary
to bracket all reference to or statements about objects of
knowledge in general, the 'real', the 'concrete', etc., as
epistemological. This does not commit us to denying that
tables exist or cause us intellectual discomfort when we
refrain from walking out of the top windows of high
buildings. The reason why discourse is interminable is
because the forms of closure of discourse promised in
epistemological criteria of validity do not work. They are
silent before the continued discourse of theories which they
can never correspond to or appropriate.

This text is organised as follows. In the first chapter,
'Discourse and Objects of Discourse', we present our critique
of epistemological conceptions of the relation between
discourse and its objects. We attempt to explain how discourse
may be conceived (and the effects on theoretical work of
conceiving it in this way) when it is not supposed that it
corresponds to or appropriates unities of being external to it
in a relation of 'knowledge'. In the second chapter, 'Genesis
and Theoretical Limitations of *PCMP*', the nature of the
project involved in *PCMP* is outlined and the various errors
and problems created by this mode of analysis are considered.
In the third chapter, 'Concepts of Mode of Production and
Social Formation', the necessity and the consequences of
abandoning the concept of mode of production are
considered; further, there is an attempt to conceptualise the
mode in which objects and problems of Marxist discourses
are formed. In the fourth and final chapter we consider the
concept of possession of and separation from the means of
production and its consequences for the analysis of class
relations.

1 Discourse and Objects of Discourse

Dominant in the critical comment *PCMP* has received have been the charges of 'formalism' and 'idealism'.[1] These charges have their source in *PCMP*'s explicit rejection of epistemological forms of conceptualisation of the relation between discourse and its objects. What is at issue in these charges is not primarily the 'substantive' concepts elaborated in the text, the concepts of the different modes of production and associated concepts, but rather the manner in which positions elaborated in discourse are held to be related to the object or objects of that discourse. We have argued in *PCMP* and at greater length elsewhere that epistemological forms of conceptualisation of the relation between discourse and its objects are untenable.[2] This chapter has two parts. Firstly, we outline the structure and effects of these forms of conceptualisation and show, in particular, that they entail corresponding forms of misrecognition of the conceptual order of theoretical discourse. Secondly, we examine the implications of a systematic rejection of epistemology for the conceptualisation of the relation between discourse and its objects. *PCMP*'s own position in this respect is far from being consistent. Its attempts to break with the epistemological rationalism of *Reading Capital* are often partial and confused, with the result that the text itself remains substantially linked to the concepts and forms of conceptualisation of *Reading Capital*. Our discussion in this chapter therefore goes beyond the positions elaborated in *PCMP* and it lays the foundations for the critique of some of those positions developed in later sections of this work.

EPISTEMOLOGICAL CONCEPTUALISATIONS OF THE RELATION BETWEEN DISCOURSE AND ITS OBJECTS

Epistemology conceives of the relation between discourse and its objects in terms of both a distinction and a correlation between a realm of discourse on the one hand and a realm of actual or potential objects of discourse on the other. These realms are distinct in that the existence of the realm of objects is thought to be independent of the existence of discourse, and they are correlated in that certain elements or forms of discourse are thought, at least in principle, to correspond to, or to designate, members of the realm of objects and their properties. The precise character of the postulated correspondence may vary considerably from one epistemology to another.   ·

In empiricist epistemologies, for example, the correlation between the realm of discourse and the realm of objects is conceived as being effected through the agency of the experience and judgement of one or more human subjects. Knowledge is therefore thought to be reducible to or, more generally, susceptible of evaluation in terms of basic statements which designate what is *given* to the experience of human subjects, sense-data, cross-sections of consciousness, the facts of observation, or whatever. Sophisticated forms of empiricism may well recognise the necessity of theoretically abstract forms of discourse which do not themselves directly designate the given, but these forms are nevertheless restricted to the function of providing the means of representation of the complex relational structure, the syntax, of the given.[3] Thus all forms of discourse are reducible, directly or indirectly, to the privileged level at which the forms of discourse do directly designate what is given to the experience of human subjects.

In contrast, rationalist epistemologies conceive of the correlation between the realm of discourse and the realm of objects as being effected in a different fashion. Whether or not it allots any role to human experience in the formation of knowledge, a rationalist epistemology conceives of the world as a rational order in the sense that its parts and the relations between them conform to concepts and the

relations between them, the concept giving the essence of the
real. There is therefore a uniquely privileged level of concepts
by reference to which all claims to meaningful discourse
may be evaluated. Kantian epistemology combines elements
of empiricism and rationalism. On the one hand there is a
uniquely privileged set of concepts (called categories) which,
since they define the essential structure of all possible
experience, cannot be derived from experience. These
concepts define the possible objects of experience while
experience itself provides knowledge of whichever possible
objects of experience are realised. Kantian epistemology
therefore operates with two privileged levels of discourse,
the discourse of experience and the discourse of the
categories, and proposes to evaluate all other discourses in
relation to them.

Now, there are several general consequences of the
epistemological postulate of both a distinction and a
correlation between two realms. Three are important for the
present discussion: two concern the existence of privileged
levels and forms of discourse and of the objects they are
thought to designate, and a third concerns the conditions in
which discourse in general and knowledge in particular are
thought to be produced. These three consequences will be
outlined below.

First, the distinction and the correlation imply that
objects which are independent of discourse must nevertheless
be conceived as existing in the form of actual or potential
objects of discourse, that is, their characteristics and
properties must be such that they can be designated in and
described by specific and determinate forms of discourse.
It matters little in this respect whether the independently
existing objects are thought to take the form of *ideas* that
may be more or less adequately *expressed* in discourse, or of
material objects that may be more or less adequately
reflected in it. The basic distinction-correlation structure
and its theoretical effects remain the same in both cases. There
are uniquely privileged levels and forms of discourse which
provide the means of directly designating the independently
existing objects. Epistemology therefore entails an ontology
in at least the limited sense that the totality of what exists

is conceived as including those objects designated in and described by the privileged levels and forms of discourse. In some cases, for example in most forms of positivist epistemology, the totality of what exists is conceived as restricted precisely to what may be described and designated in the approved fashion. In other cases the totality of what exists may be conceived as going beyond what may properly be described and designated in the privileged forms of discourse. For example, the forms of designation may be conceptualised as being essentially inadequate in the sense that the formation of objects of discourse is an effect of the intervention of forms of conceptualisation on the one hand and of independently existing objects on the other. In such cases, for example in Kant or in Weber, there is a realm of objects existing 'in-themselves', independently of all cognition, and a realm of objects of discourse. In Kant's conception, these latter objects are formed through the agency of Man's faculties of experience and cognition, while in Weber's conception the investigator carves them out of an infinite reality by means of selective criteria derived from technical or evaluative interests.[4] Knowledge of objects of discourse is therefore never able to provide a knowledge of objects as they are in themselves. Such positions are condemned as agnostic by proponents of other epistemologies because they postulate a realm of objects as existing that cannot be known through the forms of discourse.

In all epistemologies the conception of privileged levels and forms of discourse provides a touchstone against which all claims to knowledge may be judged. Discourse that is not itself an instance of a privileged level or form must be reducible to, or at least compatible with, approved discursive elements or forms if its claims to knowledge are to be taken at all seriously. Discourses which cannot pass this test do not provide knowledge: in that case they may be meaningless or in error or they may be a meaningful but non-cognitive form of discourse. In empiricist epistemologies there are thought to be basic statements which directly designate elements of the independently existing realm of objects. The basic statements designate what is given to the experience of one or more human subjects. The experience of the subject is therefore the primary medium of representation of objects, while the judgement of this subject, possibly aided by methodological rules and conventions, is necessary to ensure the adequacy of the discursive representation to the experience represented. Empiricism must therefore postulate a capacity of experience to function as means of representation and a faculty of judgement as two essential attributes of the human knowing subject. These attributes being given, then basic statements may function as means of proof, either by verification or falsification, of theories, hypotheses and other possible claims to knowledge. In rationalist epistemologies on the other hand there are thought to be privileged levels of conceptualisation that are not established in the experience of human subjects. In the rationalism of *Reading Capital*, for example, knowledge is conceived in terms of a determinate relation of appropriation between forms of discourse on the one hand and real objects that are independent of discourse on the other. The real object, independent of thought, is appropriated by means of the construction of the object of discourse (the thought-object) in the diachronic order of development of concepts. Rationalism claims to reproduce the real in the form of abstraction through the order of discourse. In *Reading Capital* the 'knowledge effect' of appropriation is supposed to work through the effects of the discrepancy between the synchronic order of the system of concepts and the diachronic order of the development of concepts in the discourse of the proof. The forms of order of discourse and the appropriation of the concrete are directly connected. In Althusser's text a scientific 'knowledge effect' is conceived as a function of a form of discourse governed by a determinate system of concepts, a scientific problematic. Each scientific problematic therefore constitutes a privileged level and form of discourse and any other form of theoretical discourse may be measured against the appropriate scientific problematic: if it is a possible discourse of the problematic then it is scientific, otherwise it is ideological. The circularity and ultimate dogmatism of all epistemological conceptions should be evident since there can be no demonstration that such-and-such forms of

discourse are indeed privileged except by means of forms of
discourse that are themselves held to be privileged.

A *second* significant consequence of epistemological
conceptions of a realm of objects existing independently of
discourse and of privileged levels and forms of discourse in
which those objects may be known is that these conceptions
provide the foundations for two modes of critique of
theoretical discourse that are quite distinct, although they
are frequently combined in particular cases. In the first mode
of critique, epistemology legitimises what might be called a
'realist' approach to the analysis of theoretical discourse.
If independently existing real objects are thought to exist
in the form of actual or potential objects of discourse, then
any theoretical discourse may be measured against what is
thought to be known of those objects. For example,
Talcott Parsons has been criticised for his alleged failure to
conceptualise such 'realities' as 'social change', 'social
conflict', the 'freedom' and 'creativity' of the human
individual, and 'bourgeois' historians and social scientists have
been criticised for their failure to recognise objects specified
in Marxist discourse, and so on. Here, far from constituting
a theoretical critique of the concepts and arguments of the
discourse in question, this mode of analysis merely measures
the substantive distance between the objects specified in
one discourse and those specified in another.[5]

With respect to the second mode of critique, if there are
privileged levels and forms of discourse, then any given
theoretical discourse not only can but must be evaluated by
reference to those privileged forms. Here the mode of
evaluation is epistemological or methodological rather than
'realist': it is concerned with the manner in which problems
are posed for and resolved in the discourse in question,
whether it follows epistemologically approved forms of
proof, etc., rather than with the particular objects of
discourse that it specifies. Thus each epistemology implies
a corresponding mode of reading and evaluation of theoretical
discourse by reference to the privileged forms which it
postulates. Whatever its own conceptual order, a theoretical
discourse must be examined for its implications with regard
to discourse of the privileged forms. Any features of the

order of concepts of a discourse that are not pertinent to such a mode of reading are of secondary importance and may be ignored while the discourse is put to its epistemological test. Each epistemology, that is to say, tends to give rise to a form of grid reading in which the order of development of concepts in determinate discourses is forced into the pattern of the grid and all features that cannot be so forced are ignored. Each epistemology therefore generates its own peculiar forms of misrecognition of the discourses to which it is applied. Empiricist epistemologies, for example, postulate the privileged character of 'observations' or 'factual' statements, basic statements which purport to represent what is given to the experience of human subjects. Theoretical discourses must therefore be read for the basic statements that may be derived from them, i.e. for their 'predictions', and those basic statements tested against the experience and judgement of suitably qualified human subjects, for example, of scientists trained in the appropriate observational techniques. The grotesque distortions of Marxism and psychoanalysis at the hands of such empiricist readings are well known. It is easy to see why *PCMP* must be charged with 'formalism' by empiricist readings. Not only does it deny that concepts of social relations formed in the text were to be applied to 'corresponding' real objects, e.g. in its rejection of antiquarianism, but, in the Conclusion, it also denied the possibility of application and therefore of a correspondence between conceptualisation and the real. (*PCMP* is by no means consistent on this last point and in the Introduction, for example, it advances a different position.) The charge of 'formalism' may then be advanced by empiricism on two separate counts: firstly, it challenges *PCMP*'s claim to construct concepts without referent, and secondly it objects to the dismissal of concepts by reference to questions of the order of concepts in discourse and without reference to the allegedly privileged order of the given.

Rationalist epistemologies on the other hand affirm the privileged character of determinate bodies of concepts - Kant's 'categories', Althusser's 'scientific problematics', etc. - and these provide the basis for a critical evaluation of

the scientific or unscientific character of theoretical
discourses in general. For example, Althusser establishes
the unscientific character of the conception of social
relations of production as intersubjective relations by
showing that that conception is incompatible with what he
identifies as the basic concepts of *Capital*. Althusser's
argument on this point has been examined elsewhere[6]
and it need not be reconsidered here. Once again it is easy
to see how *PCMP* could be charged with 'formalism' from
the point of view of the rationalism of *Reading Capital*.
We have seen that in *Reading Capital* the forms of order of
discourse and the appropriation of the real object through
the construction of the object of discourse (thought-object)
are intimately connected. Hence the separation of questions
of discursive order and the discursive practice itself from
any reference to the concrete, the denial of the appropriation
effect, must appear as the most pernicious formalism. For
Reading Capital, as for empiricism, there can be no autonomy
of theoretical discourse from the process of appropriation of
real objects in thought. We return below to the theoretical
effects of *Reading Capital*'s conceptualisation of the relation
between discourse and its objects. What must be noted here
is that all such arguments or readings of theoretical discourse
must stand or fall with the epistemology from which the
allegation of privilege is derived.

A *third* consequence of the epistemological postulate of
both a distinction and a correlation between realms is that an
epistemology must involve some implicit or explicit
conception of the conditions in which discourses in general
are produced and of the distinctive conditions of the
production of knowledge in particular. Knowledge is conceived as involving a distinctive type of discourse that is
produced as the outcome of a determinate process involving
determinate relations between a discourse-producing agency,
say a human subject or a community of scientists, and the
object or objects known in the discourse. For example,
knowledge may be represented as resulting from the
application by suitably trained human subjects of the
'scientific method' to particular real objects or as the outcome of theoretical practice, a 'process without a subject',

governed by a determinate 'scientific' problematic. It is with reference to the implicit or explicit conception of a determinate knowledge process that Althusser elaborates his general concept and critique of the empiricist conception of knowledge. In Althusser's account the empiricist conception of knowledge posits a 'subject', an 'object' and a process of abstraction that takes place between them. The 'subject' abstracts from the 'object' its essence and that essence is called knowledge. The empiricist conception of knowledge is therefore an epistemology: it posits a distinction between a realm of discourse and a realm of objects and a correlation between them that is effected in the knowledge process. Althusser's definition of the empiricist conception of knowledge is intended to subsume the whole field of classical epistemology. Thus the term 'subject' must be understood as designating whatever knowledge-producing agency may be posited by an epistemology, whether that agency be an empirical or transcendental human individual or some supra-individual agency, a scientific community, a class, a society or culture, etc.

In all cases it is clear that those attributes of the 'subject' deemed essential to its epistemological performances cannot be consistently conceived as open to investigation in the knowledge process itself, for any investigation of those attributes must presuppose their effects in the knowledge process made possible by their existence. The constitutive 'subject' of knowledge cannot also be an object of knowledge. It must therefore appear to knowledge as an absolute given - or else as given by some 'superior' form of knowledge (religion, philosophy, experience, . . .) whose claims to superiority must be accepted without hope of demonstration. Empiricist epistemologies identify the epistemological 'subject' with two essential attributes held to be characteristic of the human subject, namely, its faculties of experience and of judgement. Expiricism presupposes the capacity of human experience to function as representation and the capacity of human judgement to describe and to compare what is represented in experience. It is clear that those capacities cannot be established within the limits of empiricist epistemology, for that would entail *either* a demonstration which rests on what has to be demonstrated, namely, the capacities of experience and judgement to function as the means of designation of what is represented, *or* an attempt to theorise the subject in such a way that its attributes of experience and judgement are placed in question and another knowing subject is not supposed. The category of the subject and the problems of forms of subjectivity, human and non-human, legal and economic, and so on, cannot be seriously posed as problems for theoretical investigation within empiricist epistemology.

Now it is well known that in his own conception of knowledge, Althusser attempted to break with the subject-object structure of the empiricist conception of knowledge by conceiving knowledge as a 'process without a subject'. Far from being the constitutive centre of the knowledge process, Althusser's subject appears as the bearer of forms of social practice. In the case of knowledge the human subject is conceived as the bearer of determinate functions in a determinate process of theoretical practice, and that process is governed not by any alleged essential attributes of the subject but rather by a determinate theoretical problematic. A theoretical discourse is scientific or ideological according to whether its production is governed by a scientific or an ideological problematic. A 'scientific knowledge effect' is generated by a discourse whose produc-tion is governed by a scientific problematic, and an 'ideological knowledge effect' is generated by a discourse whose production is governed by an ideological problematic. Thus, while at one level he appears to avoid the subject-object structure of epistemology, Althusser nevertheless conceives of (scientific) knowledge as the outcome of a distinctive type of production process which has the effect of appropriation of the real object through the construction of a (scientific) object of discourse. In this conception, (scientific) knowledge is the product of a special type of discourse-producing agency constituted by the dominance of a scientific problematic. Althusser therefore retains the epistemological structure of a discourse-producing agency (a 'subject'), an object and a process that takes place between them to produce (scientific) knowledge. Once again the

essential attributes of the constitutive elements of the
(scientific) knowledge process, in this case the scientific
problematic, cannot be an object of knowledge. The
'scientific' character of a scientific problematic is
represented in his discourse as absolutely given, and
Althusser explicitly rejects the possibility of forms of
theoretical discourse in which the scientific or non-
scientific character of problematics may be established.

IMPLICATIONS OF THE CRITIQUE OF EPISTEMOLOGY

Our critique of epistemological conceptualisations of the
relation between discourse and its objects has been elaborated
elsewhere and there is no need to repeat its arguments here.
The preceding discussion has been necessary to bring out
the epistemological character of Althusser's conception of
knowledge and to establish the epistemological foundations
of the charge of formalism directed at *PCMP,* whether that
charge has been made from the standpoint of empiricism or
the standpoint of Althusserian rationalism. If epistemological
criteria of validity do not hold, then the *epistemological*
charge of formalism must collapse. A more significant
point is that if the epistemological notion of 'knowledge' is
not a necessary one, then the relation between discourse and
its 'objects' need not be represented in terms of both a
distinction and a correlation between a realm of discourse and
an independently existing realm of objects. It is then no
longer possible (in the absence of the epistemological
conception) to refer to objects existing *outside* of discourse
as the measure of the validity of discourse. On the contrary,
in the absence of such extra-discursive (and yet specifiable)
objects, the entities specified in discourse must be referred
to solely in and through the forms of discourse, theoretical,
political, etc., in which they are constituted. What is
specified in theoretical discourse can only be conceived
through that form of discourse (or another, critical or
complementary, discourse); it cannot be specified extra-
discursively. The question of the 'reality of the external
world' is not the issue. It is not a question of whether

objects *exist* when we do not speak of them. *Objects* of
discourse do not exist. The entities discourse refers to are
constituted in it and by it. The distinction and the
correlation characteristic of epistemology depend on objects
which exist independently of knowledge, and yet in forms
appropriate to knowledge itself.

Thus, for example, the concepts of different modes of
production specify distinct objects of/in discourse. They play
determinate roles in the formation of the concepts of other
discursive forms (thus, Marx used the concept of simple
commodity production to analyse the properties of capitalistic circulation, and Lenin used the concept of capitalistic
circulation to analyse the development of the home market in
Russia). The status of the entities constituted in a discourse
depends upon the problems it sets: thus, simple commodity
production may be part of a process of formation of other
concepts or a means of analysing problems of direct political
relevance. Entities do not have a *general* status as 'objects of
knowledge'. Modes of production are not representations or
appropriations of unities of being corresponding to their
concepts and yet existing independently of their concepts.

These remarks raise a number of basic issues the clarification of which is necessary at this point in order to provide
the foundations for our subsequent discussion of the
implications, with regard to Marxist theory in particular, of
the rejection of epistemological forms of conceptualisation.
Firstly, in view of our critique of the dogmatic character of
epistemology, it is necessary to insist that our arguments here
are not concerned to replace one dogmatism by another.
The dogmatism criticised above is internal to the structure of
an epistemology. To posit a correlation between a realm of
discourse on the one hand and an allegedly independent
realm of objects of discourse on the other is to posit certain
levels or forms of discourse (the discourse of experience, of a
scientific problematic, etc.) as directly effecting that correlation. Those levels or forms of discourse are therefore posited
as being epistemologically privileged. They provide the
touchstone in terms of which all other levels of discourse may
be evaluated, but they cannot themselves be subject to that
evaluation. An epistemology is a dogmatism in the sense that

it posits a certain level or form of discourse as being epistemologically privileged and ultimately immune to further evaluation. To reject epistemology is to destroy the foundations of that dogmatism. We return to the significance of this point at the end of this section.

Secondly, our denial of the independent existence of a realm of objects of discourse has nothing whatever to do with epistemological idealism. An epistemology is a form of theoretical discourse which specifies a number of objects of discourse and relations obtaining between those objects. It must specify, for example, discourses that do express knowledge and those that do not, the conditions of production of discourses, an independently existing realm of objects in the form of actual or potential objects of discourse, and it must specify relations of adequation and inadequation between elements of the realm of discourse and elements of the realm of objects. Idealist and materialist epistemologies differ not in their affirmation of the existence of a realm of objects of discourse independent of discourse itself, but rather in their conception of the character of that realm, that is, they differ over whether it is essentially spiritual or non-spiritual in character. More significant than that difference for the present argument is the point that all epistemologies share the conception of an independently existing realm of objects that may none the less be correlated with their representations or appropriations in determinate forms of discourse. *To deny epistemology is to deny that correlation. It is not to deny forms of existence outside of discourse but it is to deny that existence takes the form of objects representable in discourse.* The rejection of epistemology implies a rejection of the epistemological conception of knowledge as involving a more or less adequate representation or appropriation of some independently existing reality. It implies no affirmation that knowledge is the appropriation of some essentially spiritual reality (as in idealism) or of some essentially material reality (as in materialism), nor does it imply that knowledge is essentially inadequate to the real object known (as in agnostic epistemology). Rather it implies that the relation between discourse and its objects cannot be conceived as an epistemological relation of knowledge at all. This displacement of the conception of discourse as a form of knowledge, as the more or less adequate representation of independently existing entities, entails a corresponding transformation in our conceptualisation of the relation between a discourse and its conditions of existence. In particular, those conditions can no longer be conceptualised in terms of their interference in the know-ledge relation or of their securing that relation against interference. On the contrary, although this point cannot be fully elaborated here, it is necessary to conceive of theoretical, political and other forms of discourse as determinate forms of social practice with their own conditions of existence in other social practices (experimental, political, economic, . . .) and in social relations and as having definite effectivities with regard to those practices and relations. We shall return to the implications of this conclusion for the conceptualisa-tion of relations between theory and political practice in a later section of this work.

Relations Between Objects of Discourse

The argument that objects of discourse exist only in and through the forms of discourse in which they are specified raises the questions of how we are to conceptualise firstly the connections between objects of discourse themselves and secondly the relations between those connections and the connections between the concepts with which the objects of discourse are specified. It is clear that epistemological concepts of the relation between discourse and its objects must have serious implications for the conceptualisation of these connections and relations. On the one hand, in empiricist epistemologies objects of discourse are conceived as given in the experience of human subjects and their representation in discourse is a function of that experience mediated through the exercise of the human faculty of judgement. Connections between objects must therefore be conceived as given in experience. Hence the classical empiricist conception of these connections in terms of a mechanical, external causality representing nothing more than the existence of regular and recurrent observable correlations between phenomena. These relations must, in the final analysis, be established in and tested against the facts of observation. Connections between concepts can have only a secondary role to play in these conceptions. Thus, while some empiricist epistemologies may allow the forms of logic and pure mathematics an exceptional status, theoretically derived relations in general must always be subjected to the tests of experience. In rationalist epistemology on the other hand the world is conceived as a rational order in which the concept gives the essence of the real. Relations between concepts therefore represent the essential form of the connections between objects. Hence the classical rationalist conception of objects and connections between objects in terms of an expressive causality, an internal relation between an essence and the phenomenal forms of its expression. Here it seems that connections and interdependencies between independently existing objects may be established through purely theoretical argument. Many epistemologies, of course, are neither purely rationalist nor purely empiricist but some uneasy combination of the two. In those cases the deter-mination of the connections between objects will be subject to the competing claims of reason on the one hand and of observation on the other.

Now, if objects of discourse have no existence independent of the forms of discourse in which they are specified, then the connections between objects cannot be conceptualised in terms of either the mechanical external causality of empiricism or the expressive causality of rationalism. On the contrary, the connections between objects can only be conceived as a function of the forms of discourse in which those objects are specified; they are not empirically given to theory by the real nor are they given in the internal relations between the concepts with which the objects are specified. This means firstly that the connections between objects cannot be reduced to any universal form, whether it be the form of a mechanical causality, in which connections are thought to be given by the 'facts' of the case, an expressive causality, in which connections are given by the relevant concepts, or some combination of the two. These connections will always

be a function of the particular forms of discourse in which
the particular objects in question are specified. Secondly, as a
consequence of this first point, it follows that questions of
the relations between concepts of a discourse and of forms
of demonstration and criticism concerning questions of
discursive order should be separated from questions of the
connections between the objects specified in discourse and
from the forms of demonstration that those objects must be
conceived in the way specified. For example, specification
of the feudal mode of production must refer to forms of law
and politics affecting the relation between lord and serf.
Here one concept involves a necessary reference to another.
But the doctrine of 'determination in the last instance' goes
further than that: it maintains that there are specifically
'feudal' forms of law and politics that are themselves *effects*
of the feudal mode of production. Connections between
objects of discourse cannot be derived from internal
relations between concepts. These conditions are not easy to
satisfy and they are manifestly not satisfied in much of the
argument of *PCMP*. Failure to respect these conditions
involves a collapse into empiricist or rationalist conceptualisations of the connections between objects. These latter, in
particular, are prominent in much of Marxist theory, from
the doctrine of 'determination in the last instance' by the
economy to Althusser's sophisticated reworking of that doctrine in his conception of a structural causality governed
by the matrix role of the economy. We shall return to the
theoretical effects of the rationalism of *Reading Capital* in
a moment.

But first, in view of its significance for the objectives of
this work, it is necessary to consider the conceptualisation
of connections between objects with particular reference to
relations of production and other objects of Marxist theory.
Relations of production may be briefly specified as involving
the social distribution of the means and conditions of
production, that is, the distribution of possession of and
separation from the means of production among different
categories of economic agents. The concepts of 'possession
of' and 'separation from' the means of production are
examined in a later section of this work. For the present it

is enough to say that possession of certain means of production involves the capacity to control the functioning of those means in the process of production and the capacity to exclude others from their use except on the terms of some economic relation governing the distribution of the product of that process. Possession of certain means of production by one category of economic agents therefore entails the separation from those means of other categories of economic agents. It follows directly from this brief outline of the concept of relations of production that the specification of these relations involves the explicit or implicit reference to the *effects* of other social relations and of social practices other than economic production. For example, the specification of determinate relations of production entails a reference to agents who occupy the positions specified in those relations. It therefore pre-supposes a definite legal and cultural-ideological determination of the capacities of agents in general or of distinct categories of agents (e.g. citizen, slave, freedman, etc.) and also of what entities are capable of assuming the capacities of agents, that is, of what may or may not be a legal or customary subject (human individuals, joint-stock comapnies, religious orders, etc.). In addition it presupposes the determination and the legal or customary recognition of those specific types of capacities and obligations assignable to agents occupying determinate positions of possession of or separation from determinate means of production. These conditions include (a) legal or customary definition and sanction of rights and obligations (law of contract, property, etc.) and (b) the existence of forms of calculation consistent with the performance of the relevant capacities. This inventory of what is presupposed by determinate relations of production should be continued to include 'forces of production', since relations of production necessarily involve means and processes of production, and the particular conditions in which production does take place (the levels and forms of wage-payment, hours of labour, etc.).

However, what must be noted here is that determinate relations of production cannot be specified without an explicit or implicit reference to certain effects of other social

relations and of social practices. We shall call those effects
which are necessarily implicated in the specification of
determinate relations of production the *conditions of
existence* of those relations. To specify the social relations
and practices responsible for those effects is to specify the
form in which the conditions of existence of the relations
of production are secured. Relations of production can be
conceived only as articulated on to other social relations and
social practices, and we may define a social formation as an
object of discourse in which the conditions of existence of
determinate relations of production are secured. The
consequences of this conception of the connection between
the concepts of relations of production and social formation
are considered in later sections of this work. In the present
context it is sufficient to note that the social formation is
not conceptualised as a determinate finite unity of being
internally differentiated into levels (economic, political and
ideological) and sub-unities of being (dominant and
subordinate modes of production) and structured by
dominant and subordinate levels of effectivity governed 'in
the last instance' by the economy. It follows that the form
in which the conditions of existence of determinate
relations of production are secured cannot be conceived either
as empirically given to theory or as derivable in principle
from the relations of production whose conditions of
existence they secure. Empiricist and rationalist conceptualisations of the connections between relations of production and their conditions of existence both entail the
theoretical consequence of the non-conceptualisation of the
effects of those conditions. On the one hand, those conditions of existence are conceived as given outside of theory
and therefore as dependent in their form and action on the
circumstances of the 'case'. On the other hand, where the
conditions of existence are treated as derivable from the
concept of the dominant relations of production, those
relations are treated as determining their own conditions of
existence whose effects must then be conceived as given in
the relations of production themselves. Only rationalist
conceptualisations allow the relations of production to be
conceived as securing their own conditions of existence. An

all too common tendency in Marxist theory is to combine
elements of rationalist and empiricist conceptualisations in
such a way that whilst empirically given variations may be
recognised, the essential features of the social formation are
nevertheless thought to be determined by the dominant relations of production. Thus, features not determined by the
economy are recognised on the one hand and deemed
inessential, and therefore ultimately ineffective, on the
other.

The arguments of Althusser and Balibar in *Reading Capital*
provide an excellent example of the theoretical effects of
rationalist forms of conceptualisation in which certain
concepts and discursive forms are thought to specify objects
capable of independent existence, determinate unities of
being. In *Reading Capital* the concept of mode of production
is not conceived simply as specifying a determinate object
of discourse and as playing determinate roles in the formation
of the concepts of other objects of discourse; it is the concept
of social relations as forms capable of existence independently of the discourses in which they are specified. What
is appropriated by the concept is a unity of being complete
with its determinants and effectivities. Althusser argues that
'what Marx studies in *Capital* is the mechanism which makes
the result of history's production exist *as a society*' (p.65)
and further that 'the mechanism of production of this
"society effect" is only complete when all the effects of
the mechanism have been expounded, down to the point
where they are produced in the form of the very effects
that constitute the concrete, conscious or unconscious,
relation of individuals to society as a society' (p.66). Hence
the conditions of existence of social relations and their
effectivity as social relations are present in or deducible from
their concepts. The concept may therefore be conceived as
existence in abstraction.

In *PCMP* we argued that the effect of this conception is
to reduce the conditions of existence of social relations and
their effectivity to their connections in the order of
concepts, to assign an auto-effectivity to the relations
between concepts. Once existence is postulated, then the
modalities of that existence are given in the concept and

their effects are derivable from their conceptual forms.
Althusser and Balibar conceived modes of production as
eternities existing through the action of their structure and
they conceived forms of transition as essentially finite, as
forms generating others through the action of their internal
contradictions. The notion of the thought-object representing
the concrete in thought requires that the order of concepts
necessarily appropriates the order of effectivity of the real.
Thus there can be no discrepancy between the forms of
(scientific) knowledge and what is known by them except
as an effect of the intrusion of non-scientific, ideological
elements into the discourse.

It is this notion of the auto-effectivity of the concept that
criticisms by Poulantzas and others of *Reading Capital* for
its conflation of the concepts mode of production and social
formation are attempting to indicate in a confused and
relatively untheoretical way. Formally, of course, there is no
conflation. For Althusser and Balibar, a social formation is
the combination of a number of modes of production and
the intertwining of the structural causalities of these modes
in a hierarchy of determinations. The problem does not lie
in the failure to distinguish these concepts but in the notion
that the theory of modes of production can generate the
forms of combination which represent the social formations
that are possible. The theory of modes of production is the
basis for the appropriation of history in thought. In *PCMP*
we argued that *Reading Capital* occupies the terrain of philosophies of history and, further, that it does so at the cost of
theoretical incoherence by introducing the principle of 'non-
correspondence' to provide for the 'transitions' which make
possible the conception of history as a hierarchy of forms
(from feudalism to capitalism to . . .).

In addition to rationalising 'history', *Reading Capital*
generates a number of other theoretical effects which place
it on a level with empiricist epistemologies and their
'subjects'. Althusser argues that social formations and modes
of production must be conceived as engendering 'society
effects'. That is, while social relations involve a process
without a subject, that process requires subjects as its
'supports'. Althusser denies the place of the constitutive

subject which generates social relations as an effect of its 'praxis'. The subject is, however, necessary as a 'moment' (to use a Hegelian term) of the process. Subjects are conceived as 'agents', that is, definite functions as supports of certain structures of social relations. Since the subjects are not constitutive and are irreducible to effects of the process, that is, they remain subjects within the places generated for them by the structure, the process must be represented to them in order for them to function as agents. If the concepts are to cognise a 'society effect' (and therefore produce a knowledge effect), then this process of representation must be determinate and its conditions of existence must be given in the concept of the social relations as a whole. These conditions, non-constitutive subject as agent and systematic connection of representation with the structure, predetermine the theoretical result; this is most clearly and brilliantly represented in Rancière's paper 'The Concept of "Critique" and the "Critique of Political Economy"'.[7] The subject has represented to it phenomenal forms of the process and these forms are specific to the place occupied by the subject. The link between the forms, the subject and the place is the concept of *experience*: the subject occupying a particular place occupies a particular point of perception of the structure, a partial point which provides it with the forms of representation necessary to its function as an agent. This conception supposes a necessary and invariant system of 'places' (functions and points of perception corresponding to them) and subjects with the faculty of 'experience' and an absence of attributes so that they can become *subjects of the place*. The process is thus conceived as a necessary structure, generating places as functions which support it, and this structure is supported by introjecting into its necessity subjects as beings with attributes necessary to it (capacity to experience) but not given by it. Structural necessity is conditional upon the presumption of subjects with the attributes of the knowing subject. Far from being an anti-humanism in the sense of creating a subjectless process, Althusser's structural causality requires the concept of subject, a concept moreover which is not theorised but simply incorporated as a necessity. Althusser's later work on ideology attempts to rectify this introjection by trying to theorise the mechanism of the formation of subjects and the mechanism of their distribution to 'places'. In both respects he fails. The basically 'phenomenological' theory of the genesis of the subject constantly presupposes the subject of experience as the condition of formation of the subject, and the theory of the reproduction of the relations of production assigns a necessary 'function' and then seeks apparatuses to perform it. These questions of the theory of ideology are diversionary in the present context and we have discussed them at length elsewhere.[8] We raise them here in order to emphasise that where concepts of social relations are constructed as the concrete-in-thought, then all the conditions and effectivities of those relations must be given in thought. Forms of effectivity which are not necessary consequences of the structure subvert the structure's role as thought concretum, they threaten to problematise the relation of concepts and the concrete. Hence the necessities of the structure require non-conditional essential subjects as their conditions of operation.

General Concepts and Levels of Discourse

Finally, the rejection of epistemological conceptualisations of the relation between discourse and its objects means that there cannot be any privileged levels of discourse of the kinds postulated by epistemology. The notion that there is a uniquely privileged empirical or observational level of discourse in terms of which all other levels of discourse (theories, hypotheses, etc.) must be evaluated and rejected if they fail to conform is a consequence of empiricist epistemology and must stand or fall with the epistemology on which it is based. Similarly, the notion that there is a set of basic concepts, Kant's categories or the basic concepts of Althusser's scientific problematics, to which all other concepts must conform or from which they may be derived, must stand or fall with the rationalist epistemology on which it depends. There are no privileged 'basic concepts' of Marxism or of any other field of theoretical discourse.

Thus, Balibar's proposal that there is a set of basic concepts of historical materialism capable of generating the concepts of all possible modes of production and their combinations must be rejected as untenable. Similarly, the rejection, in *Reading Capital* and other texts, of theoretical humanism and of 'Hegelian' conceptions of history and of the structure of the social formation on the basis of their difference from and incompatibility with what were regarded as the fundamental concepts of Marxist theory cannot be defended. Inconsistency between two bodies of concepts does not in itself provide any grounds for rejecting one and accepting the other, and the notion that it does provide such grounds is the product of a rationalist conception that regards certain bodies of concepts as providing a uniquely privileged access to the real. If there are no uniquely privileged levels of forms of discourse, then no form of discourse can be evaluated, as true or false, scientific or ideological, by reference to its difference from some other form of discourse. Forms of theoretical discourse may be examined with regard to the internal structure of relations between concepts and the levels and forms of inconsistencies entailed in those relations. The results of such an examination may have serious implications for the theoretical foundations of the positions advanced in a determinate form of discourse, but they carry no implications whatever regarding the 'success' of that form of discourse in 'appropriating' or 'representing' the real.

The primary object of analysis in *PCMP* is not some independently existing set of 'pre-capitalist' social relations but rather a level of Marxist theory designated in the text as 'the theory of modes of production'. That book attempts to criticise, reformulate and develop that theory by subjecting certain conceptions of 'pre-capitalist' modes of production and social relations found in the works of Marx and Engels to theoretical analysis. A set of general concepts relating to 'modes of production' appears as both the means and the product of this analysis. General concepts function in the first instance as providing means and criteria of formation of particular concepts in the discourses which constitute and analyse the specific concepts of particular modes of production. These general concepts specify, for example, the form of combination of the relations of production and the labour process, the necessity of a non-teleological conception of reproduction, and so on. In this sense they both provide the concepts with which to pose problems and indicate certain of the conditions their solutions should meet. The specific concepts of particular modes of production, on the other hand, represent definite relations of production, labour processes and forms and conditions of reproduction. These latter concepts are specific (rather than general), not in the sense that they represent particular finite unities of being but in the sense of the place they occupy in theoretical discourse. They depend for their formation on the use of the general concepts of mode of production, etc., although they cannot be derived from those general concepts without further specification. Here the general concepts function as a means of formation of specific concepts of particular modes of production, but the formation of those specific concepts involves a level of conceptualisation distinct from that of the formation of the general concepts themselves.

Now, to say that general concepts function as a means of formation of other, less general, concepts is not to say that they function as the epistemologically privileged basic concepts of rationalist conceptualisations. The discourses in which particular modes of production are constituted and specified as objects of discourse are not simple extensions of or deductions from the general concepts. On the contrary, the difficulties encountered in the formation of concepts, the concepts formed and those which cannot be formed, may well induce a theoretical labour of transformation, revision and reordering of the general concepts themselves. General concepts have no necessary primacy in theoretical discourse and they cannot therefore serve as absolute criteria governing the formation of less general concepts. They represent *a* level of conceptualisation in discourse, not a privileged source of deductions.

Thus the development and rectification of general concepts may be an outcome of the practice of formation of specific concepts by means of those general concepts. This certainly happened in the course of working on *PCMP*. There is a considerable difference between the concept of mode of production entailed in our earliest investigations (the 'ancient' and the 'primitive communist' modes of production) and that entailed in our final ones (the 'feudal' mode of production and the transition from feudalism to capitalism). The formation of the concept of the 'feudal' mode of production and the critique of the teleology entailed in the rationalist conceptualisation of mode of production and transition in *Reading Capital* involved the introduction of new questions and concepts as a result of the specific difficulties encountered with the existing general concepts and with the specific forms of conception of 'feudalism' and of 'transition' which were our point of departure. These questions and difficulties led to a reworking of the general concepts of mode and relations of production, etc., but the consequences of that reworking were not fully appreciated when the book went to press. Some of these consequences are examined in later sections of this work. It should be clear, in conclusion, that since there can be no epistemologically privileged level of discourse and no independent order of being to which the forms of discourse should ideally correspond, this development and rectification of concepts can never be finally sanctioned.

2 Genesis and Theoretical Limitations of *PCMP*

PCMP stressed that the concepts of modes of production developed in the text were to be regarded as means in a larger process of theoretical work and not as primary objects of theorisation in themselves. These concepts were not produced as 'tools' or 'models' for application in the practices of economic anthropology or the writing of history. Why they were developed and written as they were can be understood only by reference to prior theoretical problems and, in particular, to the problems generated by and the deficiencies of *Reading Capital*. It is an attempt to overcome the theoretical impasse created by the failure of Balibar's project for a general theory of modes of production without retreating into the empiricism and pragmatism so evident in Balibar's own 'Self-Criticism'.

The problematisation of Balibar's work in 'The Fundamental Concepts of Historical Materialism' had four major sources: (i) a seminar conducted by the editors of *Theoretical Practice* on the problem of the theory of the combination of modes of production, which concluded that there could be no general 'matrix' which determined the possible forms of combination and the necessities of the structures so formed; (ii) the questions about *Reading Capital* posed to Balibar and the response to his comments by Tony Cutler (*TP* 7/8); (iii) Balibar's 'Self-Criticism' (*TP* 7/8); (iv) an unpublished paper by one of the authors on Rancière's and Althusser's theories of ideology.[9] Other criticisms, by Glucksmann, Poulantzas and Rancière, challenged Balibar's theory but they did so in ways that failed to prevent a response in its own terms, and they were open to broader philosophical and political counter-criticisms.[10] The problematisation undertaken by Balibar and *TP* had two general conclusions: (i) that the general theory of modes of production was in effect a 'structuralist' combinatory, constituting a matrix of possible modes through forms of combination (in relations of correspondence) of a number of basic elements; (ii) that 'structural causality' entailed a conception of a totality and forms of its action which involved the auto-effectivity of the concept, essence-appearance conceptualisations, and the untheorised introduction of the concept of subject. The authors agreed with Tony Cutler in rejecting the implications of Balibar's 'Self-Criticism'. Despite a brilliant and penetrating critique of his own work, Balibar had produced no basis for theoretical advance beyond the positions criticised. Balibar emphasised the importance of the class struggle and insisted that the nature and forms of relation of one 'instance' to another could not be specified in the abstract but only in relation to concrete social formations. The 'class struggle' was little more than a touchstone or talisman since Balibar could provide no new theoretical account of the conditions and forms of its effectivity; in effect it was a gestural category adding nothing to its existing and problematic status in Marxism. Balibar's position on the 'instances' led directly to empiricism; the theorisation of the nature and forms of relation of the 'instances' could not precede the recognition of their existence in concrete social formations.

In order to overcome the problems raised by this theoretical collapse, two strategies of theoretical work seemed to be possible: the first was to work directly on the reformulation of the 'fundamental concepts', and the second was to work on the reformulation of the basic concepts through the analysis of specific concepts of modes of production. We adopted the second strategy and our choice of 'pre-capitalist' modes as the means of its development was a strategic (if not entirely explicit) one. The concepts of the capitalist and socialist modes presented serious difficulties in addition to the general problem of developing the concepts of the theory of modes of production. In the case of the capitalist mode the primary obstacles were a number of complex and unsettled debates in economic theory (value, the reproduction schemas, declining rate of profit, etc.) and, most importantly, the relation of Marx to Hegelianism. In problematising *Reading Capital* it became clear that at least certain elements of the discourse of *Capital* were also at stake, in particular the whole mode of analysis of the representation of the process to the agents. In the case of socialism the primary obstacle was the virtual absence of attempts to theorise it as a mode of production. Most work on socialist production and distribution was concerned with its possibility or technical operation as an 'economy': problems of planning as economic technique, price formation and policy, incentives, and 'efficiency' relative to capitalism dominate the literature. The pioneering work of Charles Bettelheim[11] represented only the beginnings of an attempt to theorise socialist relations of production.

PCMP developed then as a method of analysis of the theory of modes of production and the supersession of Balibar by the 'back door' as it were. When we began we had no coherent theoretical defence of this strategy and no clear expectations as to its outcome. Why was a 'back door' needed at all? The answer is a simple one: the criticism of Balibar's project took a form which rendered any 'general theory' of modes of production impossible. The general theory, in which modes were formed by the differential combination of elements, appeared to make possible the generation of concepts of specific modes of production directly from the basic concepts of the theory of modes of production. Hence Alain Badiou was by no means inaccurate when he used a metaphor from mathematical formalisation, conceiving modes as 'sets' formed by the combination of the elementary categories and the general theory as the matrix 'set' of all the 'sets' possible within it.[12] The general theory contained the basis for the derivation of all possible modes. It generated a table or series of possible existences. This table, through the differential combination of its elements (modes), generated a matrix of all possible forms of social formations, conceived as combinations of modes of production. The general theory appropriated the possibilities of history in thought.

Thus all *possible* modes could be generated from the concepts of the elements which specify the general structure of the mode of production. The differential combination of those elements must produce a series of forms and the matrix thus created imposes a limit to the forms of existence of social relations as a function of the logical properties of its categories. The logical potentialities of a certain mode of discourse and the conditions of existence of social relations are systematically conflated. The possible relations of production are limited not by any determinate conditions which would have the effect of precluding the existence of other forms, but rather by the logical properties of the elements of the general theory and the number of 'places' in the matrix created by their combinations. Such a 'general theory' can only be the product of rationalist conceptualisations of the relation between discourse and its objects.

We are not pleading against Althusser and Balibar the inexhaustible greenness of life in contrast to the limited greyness of theory. The objection is not to the limit to the number of possible modes as such, but rather to the theoretical basis of that limit in rationalist epistemological conceptions of the relation between 'basic concepts' and other levels and forms of discourse. Similarly, we are not claiming that the conditions of existence of social relations are given outside of discourse to be contrasted to the internality of discourse itself. On the contrary, we are challenging Balibar's failure to specify and conceptualise those conditions of existence and to differentiate them from the logical properties of the order of discourse itself. Balibar's rationalism fails to differentiate between the logical order of development of concepts and the order of connections between the objects specified by means of those concepts. Hence, in Balibar's case, the conception of modes of production as eternities: the modes persist through the action of their structures once their existence is posited. If they exist they have a nature as existence, a unitary form of being. Existence is a mere postulate, the modes do not have conditions of existence distinct from themselves, their existence is unconditional and unquestionable.

These effects of the rationalism of *Reading Capital* have been examined in the previous section. Modes of production cannot be conceived as appropriations of the concrete in thought. They are objects of discourse existing in and through determinate levels and forms of theoretical work, and the posing of the questions which lead to the specification of particular modes involves a distinct level of theoretical work and a connection with practices other than the theoretical. The concepts of modes of production do not themselves provide the basis for the conceptualisation of social formations: the specification of the form in which the conditions of determinate relations of production are secured cannot be deduced from the concepts of those relations. The implications of these points for the conceptualisation of modes and relations of production and social formations are examined in later sections of this book. What should be noted here is that we were in no position to produce or even to recognise those implications when we began to break from *Reading Capital*'s forms of conceptualisation.

In *PCMP* we set ourselves the limited task of beginning to reformulate the theory of modes of production through working with certain general concepts (produced through the criticism of Balibar) to form the concepts of certain specific modes of production. In order to have any hope of accomplishing this task we accepted two limitations: the first was not to investigate the conditions of the posing of the questions that lead to the formation of specific modes as objects of theorisation, and the second was not to pose as problems or to attempt to construct concepts of social formations. In lieu of investigation of the conditions of formation of specific modes as objects, we accepted existing designations of modes in the works of Marx and Engels as our starting-point. Without doubt this acceptance of a point of departure has its limitations and theoretical effects. Marx's and Engels' concepts are not all of a piece; the conditions of their formation as concepts and the status of the problems which lead to these concepts are extremely variable. In the case of some conceptions this unproblematised point of departure led us into serious errors. The best example of this concerns the 'Ancient' mode of production which we shall discuss in a moment. Some of these limitations were probably inevitable. All theoretical discourse proceeds by definite forms of abstraction, that is, it involves working on problems and objects in abstraction from other significant discursive levels, using concepts and producing results which must of necessity be problematic.

Since there are no epistemologically privileged levels or forms of discourse, it follows that the products of any discourse, in this case *PCMP,* are necessarily subject to problematisation and rectification. In order to recognise the problematic character of the concept of 'Ancient' mode of production that we developed, it was necessary that the means of problematising it be produced in further theoretical work. In order to advance the problems pertaining to modes of production, definite forms of abstraction were necessary. We have outlined our limitation of our work to certain conceptions of Marx and Engels, to a few general concepts derived from the critique of Balibar which specify the conditions of formation of the concepts of modes, and the refusal to consider the problems of the concepts of social formations. These are the forms of abstraction we refer to. These conditions which limit the problems, concepts and level of analysis in *PCMP* mean that its contribution can be of value only if it forms the basis for further work which transcends those limits and problematises its starting-point.

THEORETICAL LIMITS OF *PCMP*

A. One basic clarification and self-criticism is a necessary preliminary to all the others. The reason the text theorises 'pre-capitalist' modes of production is that its theoretical strategy involves working on general problems by forming the concepts of specific modes. Nevertheless, it is impossible to read *PCMP* without noticing concepts, arguments, analyses and contributions to debates which go beyond the limits of such theoretical work. To a certain extent the specific modes of production did become objects of analysis in themselves and the text engages in historical debates in a way that clearly goes beyond the purposes of illustration and criticism. In itself this is not a problem, but it may have consequences which affect the status and content of the general theoretical work. An example of such an effect is the attempt in the Conclusion to defend the category of '*pre*-capitalist' as valid in a non-historical sense by reference to the level of development of concepts one to another. This passage has all the marks of rationalisation and its forced categories are an index of the extent to which we had accepted the notion of 'pre-capitalist societies' as a possible object of theoretical investigation in its own right. Or again, the critique of Genovese and the discussion of the Civil War, despite our careful disclaimers, does amount to an attempt to demon-strate that the concept of slave mode of production can be applied in historical analysis. The violent critique in the Conclusion of the antiquarianism entailed in the acceptance of *pre*-capitalist socieites' as an object of analysis for Marxists is, in part, an attempt to render problematic a text which could all too easily serve as the conceptual base for such practices.

B. In taking the concepts of Marx and Engels as our point of departure we necessarily failed to investigate the sources of the problems which generated those concepts. This practice was not without its theoretical effects. The best example is our construction of the concept of the 'Ancient' mode of production, following closely the analyses of Marx and Engels. This concept is criticised in the Introduction because it does not specify the difference between the relations of production on the one hand and the conditions of the representation of classes in the state and political level on the other. This was the first example of our specific investigations problematising and developing the concepts with which we had conducted them. The discrepancy between this concept and those developed in later work was evident, but we did not indicate the source of this discrepancy.

In effect we had attempted to rationalise conceptions of the social relations of Antiquity into the structure of a mode of production. Recognising this, we thought the error consisted in confusing the concepts of mode of production and social formation and we thought it might be possible to separate these categories to produce a rectified concept of this mode. In fact the error did not arise from our confusion of mode of production and social formation but from our acceptance of the very notion of 'Antiquity' itself. We had accepted as an object of analysis a form of 'historical individuality' which has its origin as an object of discourse in

forms of theory and cultural practices far removed from
Marxist theory. Why should we regard conceptions of the
Mediterranean world from the era of the formation of the
city-states to the fall of the Roman Empire as a coherent
object of theorisation either as mode of production or as
social formation? We accepted the category of 'Antiquity'
from the works of Marx and Engels without critical
consideration of the conditions of its formation as an object
of discourse. Why should the forms of representation
engendered by the forms of political and cultural unification
of the Mediterranean world by the Greeks and Romans be
accepted as defining a unitary object of investigation?
Classicists have accepted the Graeco-Roman conception in
which 'Antiquity' appears as a 'civilisation', but that is no
reason for conceiving it as one or more social formations
governed by a single mode of production. There is no more
reason to treat 'Antiquity' as a social formation than there
is to treat Africa since the era of da Gama as one. The
investigation of the mode of formation of the objects of
analysis in Marxism, how it is that problems and objects of
theoretical investigation are formed and generated, has
scarcely begun, but it is clearly an urgent theoretical task.

C. Our specification of the mode of proof in the Introduction
gave a misleading and rationalistic account of the proofs
employed, placing too much stress on the coherence of the
concepts of modes as the primary means of demonstration.
This has led to some unfortunate misunderstandings,
particularly in the case of the 'Asiatic' mode of production.
There are two levels of 'proof' of the concepts formed in
PCMP that are not adequately distinguished in the text.
We shall demarcate these forms using the case of the 'Asiatic'
mode of production, the sole example of our rejection of
the concept of a mode of production. These levels relate to
the forms of order of the discourse in which the concept is
developed and to the order of connection of the objects
specified in the concept.

(i) *Forms of order of discourse.* The concepts of specific
modes of production are developed in a definite discursive
form in *PCMP*. Concepts are problematised if the forms of

discourse do not produce consistent concepts or if they produce results which do not correspond to the conditions of formation of modes given by the general concepts employed. In the case of the 'Asiatic' mode of production the discourse generates a necessary arbitrariness in the form of a possible 'correspondence' of the relations of production with two distinct sets of 'forces of production'. In itself this might indicate nothing more than a deficiency in the initial posing of the problems, a deficiency which could be rectified by modifying the elements specified at the start of the process of conceptualising this mode or by redefining its concepts. This is in fact what we did in the case of the feudal mode of production - but only because we were able to problematise and reformulate certain of the concepts involved in this mode (possession/separation, relation of agents to the labour process, etc.). If it were merely a question of discursive incoherence there would have been no need to reject the concept of the 'Asiatic' mode of production since the introduction of theses about the specificity of the forces of production connected with hydro-agriculture could have produced a formal solution to that problem.

In his review of *PCMP* in *Critique of Anthropology*, John Taylor implies that our rejection of the concept of 'Asiatic' mode of production is largely a result of the discursive practice we had adopted - hence his introduction of the all-purpose charge of 'formalism'. He fails, however, to provide the basis for a rectification of the concept or to recognise fully that there is a second and more important part to our 'proof'.

(ii) *The conditions of existence of the objects specified in the concept.* The primary reason for our rejection of the concept of 'Asiatic' mode of production concerned the nature of the conditions of existence of the relations of production. Our basic point was that, unless hydro-agriculture or some analogous form is supposed, the units of production in question (communes, 'peasant' farms) represent forms of combination of the labour process with relations of distribution of the product distinct from those of tax/rent. The tax/rent couple does not generate a labour process subordinate

to the effects of its distribution of the means of production.
and, therefore, a mode of reproduction which reproduces the
relations of production. This combination of the reproduction of the relations with the conditions of production
depends on the effective separation of the 'direct producers'
from at least certain of the means of production. Only on the
assumption of forms of production in which the state is a
necessary economic condition of production can relations
of tax/rent be conceived as relations of production.

In the course of our analysis we questioned how it was
possible for such a state, itself a condition of existence of
the 'Asiatic' relations of production, to exist. No classes are
supposed *independent of the state machine* in the concept of
the 'Asiatic' mode. How can a state be formed which makes
possible the relation of production given by the tax/rent
couple? It cannot be formed according to the classic
Engelsian analysis since this supposes classes and relations
of production not reducible to the state. We criticised two
possible modes of explication of state formation, namely,
the conquest theory and the functionalist theory of the
necessities of hydro-agriculture. Our rejection of the 'Asiatic'
mode was primarily based on an argument about the conditions of existence of its form of appropriation as a system of
relations of production. It was not an argument about
discursive coherence.

It should be noted that we did not deny the possibility of
existence of the forms of social relations posited in the tax/
rent couple. That would involve the confusion of mode of
production and social formation. We argued that tax/rent
relations could be conceived as existing through the extension
of the domination of already constituted states to peoples
with non-state relations of production. Tax/rent might be
extracted in forms which either reinforce or weaken the
existing relations of production. But it does not contain the
means to subordinate the labour process to the forms of
distribution of the product entailed in tax/rent as a form of
appropriation of the product. Its conditions of existence are
secured independently of the labour process and it could not
therefore, be considered as the mode of appropriation of the
product specific to a mode of production.[13]

D. The rejection of the 'general theory' form of discourse, the acceptance that modes of production are concepts with a definite level of functioning in a complex process of discourse, that the general concepts used in forming particular concepts of modes are not definitive, and that the concepts of the modes serve as means of theorisation in the formation of concepts of other objects of discourse (for example, of social formations), takes us a long way from our starting-point in *PCMP,* from the conceptions of Marx and Engels and from the problems of *Reading Capital.* We have argued that our objectives in *PCMP* concerned a level of discourse designated in the text as the theory of modes of production and not the analysis of 'concrete' 'pre-capitalist' social formations. This is clearly different from the conception Marx and Engels had of their work. We have argued that specific concepts of modes and relations of production are formed with the aid of general concepts but are not deducible from them, that these specific concepts are not limited in form or number by a matrix of possible modes. This means that *PCMP* cannot offer, as *Reading Capital* claims to offer, a definitive 'theory' of modes of production. There is no way in which the concepts presented in *PCMP* could be claimed to be definitive and exhaustive. Its project implies three definite areas of theoretical development which must result in its criticism and supersession:

(i)   The rejection of the epistemological rationalism of *Reading Capital,* of 'structural causality' and the mode of discourse associated with it, entails the separation of questions of the order of discourse, of internal relations between concepts, from questions of the forms of connection of the objects specified in discourse.

(ii) The investigation of the effects on the general concepts employed in the formation of the concepts of particular modes of production of certain of the concepts formed in the text, and particularly of the arguments of Chapters 5 and 6.

(iii) The investigation of the conditions and modes of

formation of the concepts of specific modes of production and social formations.

We have discussed the first of these areas in the first chapter
of this book and the other two will be considered in the
following chapters.

3 Concepts of Mode of Production and Social Formation

PCMP is far from being entirely consistent in its conceptualisation of relations between discourse and the objects of discourse, but at many points, most especially in the Introduction, it advances the rationalist position that the theoretical elaboration of certain general concepts, the concepts of modes of production and relations of production, etc., provides the means of analysis of 'concrete' social formations - and that this is the principal justification for abstract theoretical work in Marxist theory. In effect, it suggests that the concept of social formation is a means of appropriation of 'concrete' social formations conceived as existing independently of their appropriation in thought. It is a rationalist position in that it maintains that questions concerning Marxist concepts pertinent to the analysis of 'concrete' conditions existing independently of theoretical discourse may nevertheless be settled at the level of abstract theoretical argument. In this respect *PCMP* does not depart significantly from traditional Marxist modes of conceptualising social formations in relation to other objects of Marxist theory. The classical concept of social formation, developed and elaborated in *Reading Capital,* has the following crucial features:

(i) It represents a definite existent combination of structural levels (economic, political, ideological) and modes of production that produces a determinate and distinctive 'society effect' and it has a mode of existence that makes it relatively autonomous from other existences.

(ii)   Modes of production represent sub-unities of this existence and they contribute to the 'society effect' with varying degrees of determination depending on their position of domination or of subordination.

(iii) The 'society effect' of the social formation depends on the overall reproduction of its hierarchy of determinacy of modes of production and on the forms of the levels corresponding to that hierarchy. If the hierarchy is displaced it is replaced by a new hierarchy with a new 'society effect' and a new form of social formation emerges.

(iv)   However, that change of form and of 'effect' is not a change in all the elements of the social formation; subordinate modes become dominant or vice versa, ideological forms and state apparatuses persist with varying degrees of relative autonomy. At what point such changes of form and of 'effect' involve a change in the *nature* of the social formation is open to question.

PCMP differs from this conception in two main respects. Firstly, it maintains that the concepts of modes of production are not themselves appropriations of the concrete in thought. They do not represent determinate sub-unities of being but they nevertheless function as means of construction of concepts of 'concrete' social formations. Secondly, *PCMP* rejects the notion of social formation as a hierarchical combination of modes of production. There is no double matrix of modes and their combinations capable of generating all possible social formations in thought. Thus *PCMP* differs from *Reading Capital* in the precise correlation it proposes between the order of being and the order of Marxist discourse and in its conception of the precise forms of discourse that appropriate the concrete in thought. These differences are not without their theoretical effects but they do not alter the fundamentally rationalist mode of conceptualisation of relations between discourse and its objects.

What is most problematic about these conceptions of social formation is that, as the Introduction to *PCMP* argues, the concept 'social formation' corresponds to the ideological notion 'society': 'social formation' is the Marxist equivalent of the empiricist historical and sociological conception of society-as-object. It is conceived, to use an appropriate term from the vocabulary of idealism, as a 'historical individual', a finite unity of being existing in the form of an actual or potential object of study. While *PCMP* explicitly rejects the notion of structural casuality, it does not succeed in displacing the theoretical effects of a rationalist conceptualisation of the relation between discourse and its objects. Once epistemological conceptualisations are rejected there can be no justification for the conception of social formation as historical individual. There is no basis for the conception of the unitary 'society effect' complete with an external boundary to that 'effect' and internally differentiated structural levels. Once the conception of social formation as a determinate unity of being, existence corresponding to its concept, is abandoned, then the problems of the forms of connection between the component elements of its unitary effect, the problems of empirical contingency on the one hand and of determination in the last instance on the other, must vanish.

Social formation, like mode of production and relations of production, is a *concept*. It is a concept which functions in theoretical discourse in the formation of other concepts and in the specification of determinate objects of discourse, for example, of determinate forms in which determinate relations of production and their conditions of existence are provided. The concept of a determinate social formation is not the appropriation in thought of an independently existing 'concrete' social formation, and the order of discursive formation of the concept cannot be conceived, as it is, for example, in the doctrines of structural causality and of determination in the last instance, as reflecting in thought the order of effectivity of the real. We have already shown that the rejection of the concept of the 'concrete' does not entail an epistemological idealism. In order to render the effects of this position comprehensible to the many perfectly serious people who may feel that this rejection of the concept of 'concrete' social formations leads to an ultra-idealist conception of politics, we must now explain, firstly, the relation between general concepts of Marxist theory, the concepts of relations of production, forces of production, mode of production, etc., and the concepts of determinate social formations, and secondly, the relations between the concepts of determinate social formations and political practice.

MODE OF PRODUCTION AND SOCIAL FORMATION

In writing *PCMP* we attempted to limit our analyses to a level of conceptualisation in Marxist theory which we designated 'the theory of modes of production'. This section aims to establish the problematic character of that designation and to question the status generally accorded to the concept 'mode of production' in Marxist discourse. The classical concept of mode of production outlined above and adopted with minor changes in *PCMP* presents a structure with three levels articulated in the mode of 'determination in the last instance' or 'structural causality'. The rationalist epistemological character of that conception is evident. In this section we consider first the concept of mode of production employed in our two final investigations which specified the social relations of a definite system of production and distribution, a combination of relations and forces of production in which the relations were dominant. Mode of production in this sense is not equivalent to the economic level of·the classical conception since it does not play the role of 'determination in the last instance' with regard to other social relations. It avoids many of the rationalist dangers of the classical conception since it specifies only 'economic' forms and their conditions of existence. The forms in which those conditions are secured are not given in the concept of the mode of production itself. Secondly, with regard to this articulated combination of relations and forces of production, we show that mode of production cannot be conceived in terms of the dominance of the productive forces over the relations of production. That thesis always involves a simple functionalism and a more or less sophisticated technicism. However, our critique of the thesis of the dominance of the productive forces does not, as we suggested in *PCMP,* imply the alternative thesis of the

dominance of the relations of production. Rather the connections between forms of economic class relations (relations of
production) and forms of organisation of production
(productive forces) must be conceived in terms of conditions
of existence. For example, the specification of determinate
relations of production as involving the distribution of
possession of and separation from the means of production
among different categories of economic agents necessarily
involves reference to means and processes of production,
that is, to forces of production. In that case the forces secure
certain of the conditions of existence of the relations.
Finally, we argue that the effect of limiting the analysis in
PCMP to modes of production involved the unjustifiable
restriction of analysis to an extremely limited range of
economic class relations in which there is one category of
possessing agent and one of non-possessing agent and the
consequent neglect of the problems of conceptualising more
complex forms of class relations. We therefore argue for the
displacement of mode of production as a primary object of
theorisation by a distinct type of object, namely, social
formation, conceived as a determinate form of economic class
relations, their conditions of existence and the forms in
which those conditions are secured.

The concept of mode of production employed in *PCMP*
underwent a number of changes in the course of our
investigations. Initially, mode of production was conceived
as a complex structure with three distinct structural levels,
economic, political and ideological, such that the mode of
articulation of these three levels, and the very presence or
absence of a political level, is determined by the structure of
the economic. This conception corresponds to the classical
notion of determination 'in the last instance' by the economy
as developed and elaborated in the work of Althusser and
Balibar: the economy determines whether the political level
exists at all and it determines how the levels are articulated.
The levels themselves were conceived as 'relatively' autonomous
so that the political, where it exists, and the ideological are,
to some extent, free to react back on the economy. The
economic level was conceived as an articulated combination
of relations and forces of production in which, contrary to

the position suggested in Marx's 1859 *Preface,* the relations
of production were the dominant element. Finally, in our
earliest investigation, that of the 'Ancient' mode, the precise
status of relations of production remained ambiguous since
it was conceived on the one hand as an economic relation
and on the other as extra-economic, basically political, in
form.

The rationalist epistemological character of this conception
of mode of production is evident and we need hardly repeat
our analysis of the effects of rationalist conceptualisations
here. The dangers of rationalism were largely, but not entirely,
avoided with the concept of mode of production employed
in our final investigations, of the 'feudal' mode of production
and the transition from feudalism to capitalism. Now mode
of production specified the social relations of a definite
system of production and distribution, a combination of
relations and forces of production in which the relations
were dominant, and the effects of other social relations and
practices which represented the conditions of existence of
those relations. Only 'economic' forms and their conditions
of existence are specified in this conception, while the initial
ambiguity over the status of relations of production,
criticised at length in Chapter 5, vanishes as a result of the
distinction between 'economic' relations and their conditions
of existence. This concept of mode of production is not a
structure of combination of three, or two, instances. In the
Althusserian concept the nature of the political and
ideological levels is given by the combination: to the
economy 'corresponds' definite political relations and forms
of representation of men's relations to their conditions of
existence. Mode of production in *Reading Capital* is the
concept of a social totality. It can be seen that our final
concept of mode of production is not equivalent to the
'economic' level of Althusser's conception since it does not
have the double role which Althusser assigns to the economy,
present as an instance *in* the combination and determinant
'in the last instance' *of* the combination. The double-role
conception of the economy is possible only when mode of
production designates a social totality, where the combination results in an actually or potentially existing system of

social relations. Once social relations are conceptualised in terms of their conditions of existence, it is clear that the forms in which those conditions are provided cannot be derived from the concepts of the social relations themselves. From the concepts of economic relations no definite form of state, of ideological practices and apparatuses, can be deduced. These forms can be developed only in the concepts of determinate social formations. The conditions of existence of relations of production only give the effects necessary to the specification of those relations but they cannot determine the forms in which those effects are secured in other social relations and social practices.

Now consider the articulation of relations and forces of production in our conception of mode of production. In Chapter 5 of *PCMP,* feudal relations of production are conceived as the forms and conditions of definite class struggles. The dominance of the relations over the forces is conceived by representing the space of forms of relation of the agents to the labour process as a process of production and of appropriation. Forms of this dominance are conceived in terms of possible forms of struggle between agents and their effects. Those effects are not *produced* by the concepts of the forms, they are *represented* by them. The two concepts do not designate entities 'relations' and 'forces', one of which hegemonises the other; rather they are used to generate concepts of social relations, labour process, class struggles, etc. In those concepts, relations and forces are combined. To a considerable extent this chapter does meet the conditions of the separation of the order of development of concepts in discourse from those of the order of connection of the social relations specified in terms of those concepts - although there remains a tendency to derive class 'interests' directly from the concept of the relation of agents to the labour process.

It has been suggested that our rejection in *PCMP* of the notion of the dominance of the 'productive forces' rests heavily on their identification with technique and that a non-technicist concept of the forces of production as *social* relations might produce concepts of modes of production which parallel and differ from the ones we have advanced

by positing the dominance of the productive forces.[14]
We shall explain here our specific objections to this position
which are independent of our general rejection of the concept
of necessary dominance. These points will also illustrate
why we indicated the need for the *discursive priority* of the
relations in the Introduction to this text.

How are the concepts of the 'forces' to be designated except
by conceptualising processes of production in terms of
technique and mode of organisation of production? If a
simple technicism is avoided, then this procedure will involve
the conceptualisation of modes as based on distinct forms
of organisation of the labour process. Divisions of the labour
force into classes of agents and forms of distribution of the
means of production must be conceived as consequences or
effects of the forms of production organisation. Types of unit
of production and social division of labour between units will
be the basis of differentiation of modes of production.

An analysis of this kind would find it hard to differentiate
between capitalist and socialist systems of production without
introducing the effects of production relations. Both entail
advanced technical forms, factory organisation of production
and a developed division of production into branches.
Socialism and capitalism would probably be differentiated on
the basis of the co-operative organisation of the labour
process under socialism and the interdependence of sectors
such that planned direction and non-commodity forms of
distribution were necessary conditions of its operation. If
planning is considered a 'force of production' under socialism,
it is difficult to see how its operation can be conceived as
a technical necessity independent of the transformation of
and the struggle to transform capitalist production relations.
It is only by conceiving socialism either as an economic
necessity given a certain level of development of the
productive forces in capitalism - with the class struggle
'realising' this necessity through the effects of the contradictions it generates - or as something to be constructed merely
by developing the productive forces, that planning can appear
as a force of production not subordinate to definite production relations.

In fact the thesis of the dominance of the 'forces' always

involves the notion of the 'correspondence' of the relations
to the forces. The thesis that production relations correspond
to the necessities involved in the level of development of the
forces entails a simple functionalism. It renders inexplicable
any operation of the relations of production which has the
effect of not distributing the conditions of production so as
to reproduce the forces. The sole explanation that can be
advanced for non-correspondence is the auto-development of
the forces themselves: these forms of development induce
non-correspondence by making once necessary relations of
production obsolete - and class struggle is then called into
play to restore correspondence. Even if the most vulgar
forms of technicism are rejected in favour of a conception of
the productive forces as social relations, these forms of
technicism are ultimately required to give the thesis of the
dominance of the forces theoretical consistency. It should be
noted that the thesis of the dominance of the forces involves
the derivation of the effects of social relations directly
from their discursive forms. The effectivity of the forces must
induce either a necessary 'correspondence' between production and its economic forms or the transformation of those
forms because of their non-correspondence.

But if mode of production cannot be conceived in terms of
determinate forms of combination of one object with another
object, of determinate 'relations of production' on the one
hand combined with determinate 'forces of production' on
the other, then the pertinence of the concept 'mode of
production' within Marxist theory must itself be called into
question. If relations of production are conceived as involving
the social distribution of the means and conditions of production between classes, that is, the distribution of possession of
and of separation from the means of production among
different categories of economic agents, then the specification
of determinate relations of production necessarily involves an
explicit or implicit reference to determinate means and
processes of production, that is, to determinate 'forces of
production'. The 'forces of production' provide certain of
the conditions of existence of the relations of production in
question. The specification of determinate 'forces of production' must therefore be included in the specification of the

forms in which the conditions of existence of a determinate
set of relations of production are secured. Thus if mode of
production is not conceived in rationalist form as a necessary
combination of distinct objects, then the concept 'mode of
production' is entirely redundant. *Either* the articulation of
'relations' and 'forces' of production is conceived in terms
of the connection between social relations and the forms in
which their conditions of existence are realised, *or* it must
be conceived in terms of some kind of necessity in which the
character of one object of discourse, the 'relations' or the
'forces', is deducible from the concept of the other. The first
alternative means that there is no reason to posit 'modes of
production' as distinctive objects of analysis in Marxist
theory, while the second leads directly into the quagmire of
rationalist conceptualisations of the relations between
distinct objects of discourse.

We can now specify the limitations involved in the positing
of 'the theory of modes of production' as a distinctive level
of Marxist conceptualisation. *PCMP* advanced a critique of
rationalist conceptions of mode of production and it proposed
a conceptualisation of the dominance of relations of production in terms of determinate forms of economic class
relations. The effects of our critique are not, as we suggested
in *PCMP*, the displacement of one conception of mode of
production (dominance of the forces) by another (dominance
of the relations) but rather the displacement of mode of
production itself as an object of analysis. Mode of production
must be replaced by a distinct type of object, namely,
determinate sets of relations of production, conceived as
determinate forms of economic class relations, their conditions of existence and the forms in which those conditions
are provided. Mode of production, in other words, is displaced
by social formation as an object of analysis. Our failure to
effect that displacement in *PCMP* involves firstly the
unjustifiable restriction of analysis to those extremely
limited forms of economic class relations characterised by
only one category of possessing agent and one category of
non-possessing direct producer, and secondly, the consequent
neglect of the problems of conceptualising the conditions of
more complex forms of class relations defined by the com-

binations of distinct relations of production. In particular, there is no consideration in *PCMP* of the possibilities of the existence of class relations through the conditions of distribution of means and conditions of production entailed in the social relations of a social formation. The significance of these points will become clearer in the final chapter of this work where we examine the concepts of class and of the possession of and separation from the means and conditions of production. Concepts of relations of production and forces of production therefore function as means of formation of the concepts of determinate social formations. The concept of a social formation specifies the forms in which the conditions of existence of determinate relations of production are provided. It is not a combination of modes of production in the Althusserian sense, a kind of meta-combination of instances. The conceptualisation of social formations involves the following levels of theorisation in addition to the conceptualisation of relations of production themselves:

(i)   The specific means and processes of production, the forms of distribution of the products and the relation of those forms to the conditions of reproduction of the production processes (e.g. the concept of a social formation in which feudal production supplies capitalist producers with raw materials through long-distance trade controlled by merchant capitalist monopolies).

(ii) Forms of class relations specific to the structure of the social formation (this question is discussed in Chapter 4 below).

(iii) Forms of state and political apparatuses.

(iv) Specific cultural and ideological forms (e.g. forms of calculation employed in political practice or in the organisation of production).

(v)   The conditions for the transformation of certain of these economic, political and cultural/ideological forms (e.g. conditions of transition from capitalism to socialism).

(vi) Forms of relation to other social formations.

At most the concept of a determinate social formation specifies the structure of an 'economy' (forms of production and distribution, forms of trade, conditions of reproduction of these forms), forms of state and politics and forms of culture and ideology and their relation to that economy, economic classes and their relations, and the *conditions* for a transformation of certain of these forms. It does not designate a social totality with its necessary effectivities given in its concept, nor, as a consequence, particular 'states' of the action of such a totality or of its 'resolution' into some other form of totality. Neither the persistence nor the supersession of the economic, political or cultural/ideological forms can be deduced from the concept of the social formation in which they appear. In particular, the social formation cannot be resolved into the classical Marxist formula of economic base and its political-legal and ideological-cultural superstructures. Legal and political apparatuses and cultural or ideological forms provide the forms in which the conditions of existence of determinate relations of production are secured, but they are not reducible to their effects and they are not organised into definite structural levels which merely reflect the structure of an underlying economic base. This means that political forces and ideological forms cannot be reduced to the expressions of 'interests' determined at the level of economic class relations.

CONCEPTS OF SOCIAL FORMATIONS AND POLITICAL PRACTICE

The concepts of social formations require definite political and theoretical problems as the means of their development. In Marxist theory, concepts of modes of production have been developed on the basis of problems arising from very diverse sources and with diverse means of representation as problems: the historian's practice; the process of theoretical exposition (e.g. the concept of simple commodity production in *Capital*); political ideologies (socialism, communism); etc. Likewise for social formations: Lenin's work for *The Development of Capitalism in Russia* combines political debates and theoretical positions related to them (Narodnism,

legal Marxism), 'information' gathered by politically spon-
sored practices (*zemstvo* statistics), and a rigorous reading of
Capital. These problems created by politics and by other
forms of theorisation require theorisation and problematisation in Marxist theory. The mode in which questions are
formed and then theorised depends on the level of development of both politics and theory, and on the extent to which
they are inscribed one in the other. One undoubted consequence of the weakness of the Left in this country, its lack
of engagement with existing politics and political forces, its
doctrinaire gesture politics, its lack of political theory, is the
weakness of development of problems for theorisation.

The concepts of social formations are ·not *applied* to
'current situations'. That concept, which Althusser developed
from Lenin, played a vital role in *For Marx,* it served to pose
the need for an anti-essentialist concept of totality in
Marxism which would do justice to the complexity of
Marxist political practice and its 'object'. Althusser made the
discrepancy of the existing conceptions of Marxist theory
from Lenin's practice a *problem*. He attempted to resolve
that problem by making Marxist theory (after the break) ever
always appropriate to the practice of Lenin. The problem is
resolved by displacing it on to the terrain of the Marx/Hegel
relation, differentiating from Hegelian essentialism a Marxist
'dialectic' 'present in the practical state' in Marx, Lenin and
Mao. The system of this 'dialectic' is elaborated in *Reading
Capital.* For all the criticisms Althusser's work has received,
the central problems about the nature of Marxist theory and
politics that formed his starting-point will not go away. The
critique of essentialism (humanist, historicist, economist) and
the failure of Althusser's own attempt to transcend essentialism make the problem *inescapable.* Far from harping on
the 'unity of theory and practice', it is necessary to
investigate the forms of connection and interpretation of
those practices. Once the notion of knowledge as appropriation of or correspondence to 'being' is displaced, then
Marxist theory can have no domain of 'application'
independent of political practice. Once the notion of a form
of being which sets its own limits in its existence and is
present in the form of its concept is displaced, then the

nature of the 'objects' confronted by Marxist theory and
politics becomes problematic.

The concepts of social formations provide a theorisation
of the forms and conditions in which production and distribution, class struggles and political practices are effective.
These concepts are a means of conception of effectivities, of
the movements of production and distribution, class struggles
and politics. It would be absurd to attach the label 'concrete'
to those practices and struggles since 'concrete' is a category of
an appropriation/correspondence relation of knowledge. The
knowledge relation makes the effect and knowledge of it
distinct existences: knowledge appropriates/corresponds to
the effect, it interiorises the effect *within knowledge* while
conceiving it as *the known,* a thing whose essential nature
exists as it is beyond knowledge. We shall assert what must
appear an 'outrageous' thesis to all those who are committed
to epistemological conceptualisations of the relation between
political calculation and its objects, namely, *that there can
be no 'knowledge' in political practice.* This follows directly
from our critique of epistemology. In political practice the
conditions of calculation of effectivity and of the production
of effect are not separable. Political practice involves the
calculation of effect, of the possibilities and results of
political action, and that calculation rests on political relations
which condition the degrees of certainty of calculation and
the range of the calculable. Even in Marxist politics there can
be no one form of political calculation for the simple reason
that there is no one form of the political conditions of that
calculation. For example, calculation for parties committed
to parliamentary and legal struggles has quite different
conditions from those of parties engaged in directing people's
wars.

We shall return to the practice of Lenin to illustrate this
conception. It would be tempting to suggest that the greater
the capacity for effectivity of the calculating agency, the
greater the certainty of its calculations. That would be a gross
misreading. It reduces political practice to 'action' and calculation to the planning or realisation of 'action'. It implies a
dirigiste and statist conception of politics. At the end of his
life Lenin produced a series of condensed, fragmentary and

yet brilliant texts: 'On Co-operation', 'Pages from a Diary', 'Our Revolution', 'Better Fewer, But Better'. These texts insist that the development of 'socialist' relations of production in Russia depended on the political and economic development of 25 million peasant families.

The state and party could at best provide forms, conditions and means in which and by which that development could take place. They could not direct it or plan it, let alone produce it by the actions of state power. The political and economic means to determine or calculate the directions of economic development in the countryside did not exist. Given the weakness of penetration of the party among the peasantry and the 'statisation' of relations with them, there was no possibility of producing a political class analysis or analysis of forms of economic differentiation which was not suspect, which did not entail the political/bureaucratic calculations by subordinate state functionaries of the effects of their reports and actions. The political conditions of calculation imposed on the central apparatus a relation to the countryside having the form of 'knowledge', a political separation which reduced the peasantry to an 'object'. In conditions where such a separation did not exist, then this relation of 'knowledge' would be shattered: the conditions of the peasantry are not 'known', they are represented by the peasantry themselves, by the forms of political calculation and practice of the people. Relations here take the form of political dialogue within and between levels of political practice and not a relation of 'knowledge' between theory, however political, and its 'objects'.

Another metaphor may tempt the unwary in relation to this notion of calculation, namely, the conception of political practice as the 'experimental' inscription of Marxist theory in the concrete. In this conception, politics is the *phenomeno-technics* of theory, the forms of materialisation of theory. Theory is here conceived as the *rational* form of the real, as a knowledge which generates in thought the *possible* forms of being and not merely those which currently exist. The knowledge of possibility is complemented by a specific knowledge of actuality and by the selection of the means most appropriate for the realisation of theory in the current situation. Theory is therefore conceived as the source of strategic direction and politics as an instrument of knowledge. This is a seductive but absurd conception which degenerates into a political *dirigisme* or an absurd rationalism.[15]

Those with a knowledge of psychoanalytic theory may find that our conception of the relation between theorisation and calculation is better expressed in the following metaphor. Theory is not applied to the concrete in a relation of 'knowledge'. Similarly, psychoanalytic theory is not applied in analysis to 'know' and 'uncover' neuroses. The idea that analysis is a relation of knowledge imposing the truth of the unconscious upon consciousness is a classic misreading of Freud. Firstly, it reduces sexuality to an object known and the analyst to a technician of knowledge. Secondly, it involves a simple rationalist conception of knowledge as enlightenment. This misreading denies transference by confining sexuality to a 'problem' of the analysed subject. Transference destroys the notion of analysis as a relation of 'knowledge'; it is a relation in which the displacement of sexuality and the displacement of that displacement is what is at stake. It is a social/sexual relation in which the analyst is as much at stake as his client. The 'products' of this practice generate in turn problems for theory, the theorisation of those problems inducing transformation in theory. Freud's theoretical work is inconceivable in separation from the practice of analysis.[16]

If we conceive political calculation as a practice with political conditions and without privilege of epistemological guarantees (in which 'success' can furnish no 'proof' of calculation since there is no *end* to be realised), that is because it is only in this way that the question of the relations between 'theory' and political 'practice' can begin to be theorised. There is no single relation and the form of relation is not a matter of theoretical or political choice for it has its own theoretical and political conditions of existence. Politics and political calculation generate problems for theory and theoretical forms provide means, whose value is variable, for calculation. The concepts of social formations are one such means. Politics is not, of course, the only source of 'problems' for Marxist theory. Problems in Marxist theory have been generated by a whole range of discourses and practices: philosophy, the historian's practice, sociology, etc. These 'problems' should not be despised and rejected *a priori* - but they cannot be accepted on their own terms. These remarks should not be taken as definitive, they are an attempt to extend the enigmatic last pages of *PCMP*. It should be clear that our position is neither a scientism nor an ultra-idealism. Our rejection of the category of the 'concrete' is not intended to induce a retreat into the contemplation of disembodied forms. It stresses the limits of Marxist theory and the centrality of the political in relation to it. Marxism is not a scientism.

4 Classes and Relations of Production

In Chapter 5 of *PCMP* on the 'feudal' mode we extended and developed the concepts of 'possession of' and 'separation from' the means of production as they applied to this mode, although we did not fully recognise the consequences of our position. Similarly, whilst we distinguished between mode of production and social formation and argued that the concepts of modes of production did not represent sub-unities of being of the greater unity of the formation, we did not attempt any analysis of the conditions of existence of economic class relations other than those represented in the concepts of modes of production themselves. As a result of this limitation we neglected to investigate the problems of conceptualising the conditions of more complex forms of class relations and we concentrated instead on relations between a single class of possessing agents and a single class of non-possessing direct producers. In this chapter, drawing on work in process,[17] we attempt to remedy some of the effects of the limitations of our analysis of classes in *PCMP*.

POSSESSION OF AND SEPARATION FROM THE MEANS OF PRODUCTION

The concepts of 'possession of' and of 'separation from' the means of production are central to the analysis of economic classes. Economic classes have been defined in Marxist theory by the relations agents have to the means of production, and these relations are constituted by definite social relations of production. Engels insisted that classes can only exist on the basis of private property ownership of the means of production. In *PCMP* it is argued that such ownership, if it is to be an economic relation rather than a mere juridical category, and if it is not to involve the problems of 'exploitation' based on coercive relations between non-labourers with no function in the process of production and the direct producer, must be based on the effective possession of the means of production. Effective possession is the capacity to control the functioning of these means in the process of production and the capacity to exclude others from their use. The nature of these 'capacities' is therefore central to the analysis of classes.

Classes depend upon a relation of effective possession of the means of production. The logic of this proposition is clearer if it is inverted: *the existence of economic classes rests on the effective separation of certain of the agents from certain of the means of production as an effect of definite relations of production.* Classes exist where the form of possession by a definite category of agents entails the separation and exclusion of another definite category of agents from means of production necessary to them. *Possession in separation* is therefore the crucial concept for the analysis of classes: the modes of possession, of separation, and the forms of what is exclusively possessed will differentiate types of class relations. Clearly, the form of separation characteristic of capitalist production is not the general form. In general it is only *certain* of the means of production which are exclusively possessed and are denied to others to whom they are necessary conditions of production, denied except on the terms of an economic relation of payment for their use.[18] Class relations do not merely concern the separation/exclusion of *labourers* from the means of production; for example, petty commodity producers or capitalists may confront classes who exclusively possess *certain* of the necessary means of production.

Thus landlords may confront capitalists as a definite class by reason of their exclusive possession of a finite and necessary condition of production (for farmers and indus-trialists alike); this possession is effective through the com-petition of captialists in the market for the rental of land and is supported by a definite connection of the landlord class

with the state apparatus (defence of landed property by legal
and economic forms, e.g. the Corn Laws). Landlordship is
not a necessary consequence of the capitalist mode of
production (CMP), it arises from the social relations of
definite social formations. Similarly, petty commodity
producers may confront forms of merchants' capital which
provide the conditions of these producers' insertion into a
social division of labour by means of long-distance trade.
This position gives merchant's capital control of the conditions of realisation of the commodities produced. Again,
this form of dominance of merchant's capital is not a necessary consequence of all forms of petty commodity production, it depends on a specific social division of labour
established between definite social formations under
particular conditions of exchange.

These examples illustrate the point that the possession in
separation of *certain* of the 'means of production' is sufficient
(under definite social conditions) to provide the foundation
for economic class relations. These examples also illustrate
the need to specify clearly what is entailed in the general
concept 'means of production'. In consequence we shall
define the concept of 'means of production' as follows, as:
*all the conditions necessary to the operation of a particular
labour process which are combined in the units of production
in which that process takes place.* If any of these conditions is
exclusively possessed by a definite category of agents, and
the agents who direct or operate the labour process are
separated from them, then such relations provide the basis
for class relations. (Later we shall differentiate between two
types of class relations on the basis of the relation to the
labour process established by exclusive possession.)

*This definition of the 'means of production' indicates that
relations between the 'unit of production' or 'enterprise' and
the systems of circulation or distribution of the conditions of
production must be analysed if class relations are to be
rigorously determined.* This analysis must be conducted for
the concepts of the social relations of specific social
formations. Analysis of classes thus necessarily requires
the *theorisation* of units of production and of their modes
of articulation with the social relations of distribution of

the means of production and of the product of these
means.

Depending on the nature of the relations of production,
the forms of distribution of the conditions of production to
the units of production may be the locus of class relations.
A division of social labour[19] which operates through
commodity circulation will in general have the consequence
that units of production may obtain the means of production
through simple sales and purchases; exchanges are the
distribution of forms of *possession* different in content.
Where, however, a definite category of agents monopolises
the means of circulation for a category of units of production, as in our example of merchant's capital and long-
distance trade, then it may have a control amounting to
effective possession of certain of the means of production.
This may be so if the conditions of production depend
upon the realisation of the product circulated. If so, then
merchant's capital can impose its prices for reasons additional
to the discrepancy between its purchases and sales; it con-
trols through its monopoly interdiction of circulation the
reproduction of the means of production (successive sales
and purchases being the production-realisation-reproduction
cycle for the petty producer). Here a limited social division of
labour and the commodity relations corresponding to it
provide the foundation for class relations. Successive cycles
of sales and purchases reproduce the control merchants'
capital exercises over the conditions of production; the
petty commodity producer obtains them under conditions
which subordinate him to the terms of exchange imposed by
merchant's capital. Hence struggles for 'free', i.e. non-
monopoly, trade have often been at least in part class struggles.
Merchant's capitalist monopolies allied with absolutist or
capitalist states have used state power and their own armed
force to suppress independent capitalist traders and the
development of competitive market realtions. *Class relations
stem from the mode and terms of combination with the means
of production imposed upon the separated non-possessor.*

In the analysis of what the means-conditions of production
are and the forms of their possession and distribution it is
essential to avoid the economistic reduction of these forms

to technique and the concentration of analysis on the immediate forms of the labour rpocess. It is necessary to abandon the forms of economism which make the process of production essentially prior to and determinant of circulation and distribution. However, not all relations of circulation and distribution are the locus of class relations. To constitute class relations the interdiction of circulation/distribution must control necessary conditions of production and the effect of the cycle of production/distribution must be to reproduce this capacity of control in the hands of a definite category of agents.

It follows that a crucial part of the analysis of the class relations in a social formation is a theoretical analysis of the division of social labour, the mode of articulation of production with the distribution of the conditions of production, and an analysis of the characteristic forms of unit of production. The social division of labour and therefore class relations cannot be fully determined without theorisation of these forms. The social relations of production cannot in general be conceived solely as the relations between the 'direct producers' and their 'exploiters' (the agents who appropriate the surplus product from the direct producer). This is a major defect of the mode of analysis followed in *PCMP* since in that text all other class relations are considered as auxiliary or secondary. Hence the failure of *PCMP* to consider or theorise petty commodity production, merchant's capital, etc., and to analyse forms of reproduction process. These points confirm the argument of Chapter 3 of this book concerning the necessity of displacing mode of production as a primary object of analysis and of replacing it by social formation conceived as a determinate form of economic class relations, their conditions of existence and the forms in which those conditions are provided.

LABOURER AND NON-LABOURER

Our analysis in *PCMP* concentrates, where it concerns class societies, on the relations between the 'direct producer' ('labourer') and the 'exploiter' ('non-labourer'). The category of 'non-labourer' is retained from Balibar's analysis in *Reading Capital*. But the analyses of the slave and feudal modes of production render this notion confused and problematical. What are 'non-labourers'? This category must be problematised if it is not to obscure the relationship between the division of functions technically necessary to an economy (the technical division of labour) and the forms of possession of and separation from the means of production defined by the relations of production (the social division of labour). It is necessary to replace the distinction between labourer and non-labourer by a more complex conception of the relations between technical functions and possession. The connection between the social and the technical divisions of labour may be stated schematically as follows:

(i) The distribution of certain technical operations (direction, co-ordination, supervision, manual labour) is a consequence of the exclusive possession of the means of production by certain economic agents. However, to say that the distribution of these functional tasks is governed by relations of production is not to say that the tasks of, say, co-ordination and manual labour are necessarily performed by members of different classes. The differentiation of functional tasks is also an effect of the division between mental and manual labour and of the existence of particular forms of managerial organisation - and these are not reducible to any simple effect of class relations. Thus capitalists may employ specialist managerial agents who are no less separated from the means of production than the manual labourers whom they direct.

(ii) The means and conditions of production are distributed to units of production in a manner which provides the foundation for the monopolisation by a definite category of agents of certain of these conditions and thereby for the control they exercise over production.

The connection of possession and function, that certain

functions are occupied as a consequence of possession and others as a consequence of the separation associated with it, makes possible a rigorous specification of the social division of labour. It does not follow that agents who possess in separation certain of the means of production have no place in the technical division of labour; rather the occupancy of places in it is as a function of the social division. *Forms of possession which involve a corresponding separation may result (depending on the means of production possessed) in the distinction of the function of the direction of the means of production from other functions and the dtermination by the possessor of the occupancy of that function.* Thus, for example, co-ordination, a technically necessary function in any process of production combining various activities to a single end, is a function that devolves on to the capitalist or his agent in the CMP.

The technical division of labour is conditioned by the social relations of production, in the sense that it is the relations between the agents which create the conditions of existence for certain forms of technical division of labour (an example is the forms of organisation of the labour process which are connected with slave relations of production; see *PCMP,* Chapter 3). However, the places created in this socially conditioned technical division are necessary places, functions necessary to the relation of production and circulation, or to the process of production as a complex of phases and techniques. It follows that agents like capitalists and slavemasters may perform technically necessary functions within the forms conditioned by the relations of production; they are not pure 'exploiters' without economic function. Their control of the product is a function of their control or direction of the process of its production.

The 'non-labourer's' activities (a function of the articulation of the technical and the social divisions of labour) materially affect the forms and level of production and do not merely appropriate a portion of a given labour product as the 'surplus product'. Thus, for example, a feudal landlord (the 'improving' feudal landlords are classically the monastic orders) can maximise the proportion of the estate devoted to demesne land, organise production on it more rationally than the tenants on their own plots, and closely supervise the labour services performed by the tenants; by these actions the product on the demesne land is increased.

The notion of the 'non-labourer' obscures what is central in class forms of articulation of the social division of labour with the technical. Functions annexed to certain categories of agents as a consequence of possession have a real effectivity on the process of production. The category 'non-labourer' hides what the possessor does, he directs the means of production he possesses in the service of an exclusive possession. Where possession confers the capacity to direct the labour process, the 'non-labourer' and his agents occupy the pivotal positions in the technical division of labour and separated agents secondary ones. Appropriation of the product depends upon the possession connection and not on the labour contributions of the agents; where the possessor directs the labour process he nevertheless occupies a technically necessary function which enables him to direct that process in the service of that possession. All appropriation as the consequence of an exclusive possession requires at least a minimum level of direction of the means of production possessed.

All class relations depend upon forms of possession which are also forms of separation, and as a consequence combination with those means of production involves either the payment of a portion of the product for the capacity to use them, or the performance of subordinate functions in a process of production directed by the possessor. These forms of possession are sanctioned, provided with their political conditions of existence, by the state, but they rest on relations of production which reproduce the relations of possession and separation. The analysis here generally confirms the position argued in Chapter 5 of *PCMP* that class relations are economic relations, relations which are represented in the political and not forms of domination deriving from it. Far from differentiating between class relations based upon domination and those based upon economic forms, a quite different differentiation of types of class relations will be proposed here. This will be based on the relation between possession and function. The two types of class relations are the following:

(i)   Where possession of certain of the means of produc-
      tion confers upon the possessing agent the capacity to
      direct the labour process and where the separated
      agent is combined with those means in a capacity
      subordinate to this direction.

(ii) Where possession of certain of the means of produc-
      tion confers upon the possessing agent the capacity to
      determine certain of the conditions of direction of the
      labour process, but in which its direction is a function
      of the possessor of other of the means of production;
      examples would be merchant's and usurer's capital,
      and certain forms of landlordship.

The two categories are not exclusive; for example, a
capitalist farmer may employ wage labourers and operate under
the conditions of rental, maintenance and performance
imposed by a landlord. They differ in the role the possessing
agent plays in relation to the labour process. The second
type rests on the economic subordination of *directors of
the labour process,* that is, where relations of distribution
of the conditions of production are such that forms of
exclusive possession interpose themselves between these
relations and the labour process.

As Marx makes clear in the *Critique of the Gotha
Programme,* the distribution of the product is a consequence
of the distribution of the means of production and not a
function of the labour contributions of the agents. The
distribution of the means of production enables the 'possessor'
to effect a definite form of appropriation of the product
which requires of the 'possessor' a definite level of direction
of the means of production sufficient to retain effective
possession. Direction is thus a function which fuses elements
of the social and technical division of labour. For example,
Marx argues that the capitalist performs the technically
necessary function of co-ordination; he calls it 'a productive
job, which must be performed in every combined mode of
production' (*Capital, III,* p.376). 'Non-labourer' is a notion
which recalls the petty-bourgeois philosophies of labour which
Marxism attempted to displace, gospels of work and ultra-
egalitarian notions of an equal distribution of the fruits of

labour. The 'non-labourer' performs definite functions which are technically necessary to production.

This interdependence of the technical and social divisions of labour returns us to the argument of the preceding chapter, namely, that the specification of determinate relations of production necessarily refers, implicitly or explicitly, to determinate means and processes of production and therefore to the determinate technical functions necessary to the existence of those processes. There are not two distinct 'objects', 'relations of production' (the domain of the exploiting 'non-labourer') and 'forces of production' (the domain of the exploited labourer). There can be no independent evolution of the 'forces of production' outside the limits of the relations of production in which the conditions of existence of those 'forces' are provided, and no necessity of social transformation inherent in the concept of the forces of production itself. The doctrine of the primacy of the productive forces as the motor of history can be advanced only on the basis of an untenable rationalist conceptualisation of the relations between the objects of Marxist theory. We have argued that social formations must be conceptualised as consisting of a set of relations of production, their conditions of existence and the economic, political and ideological/cultural forms in which those conditions are provided. Neither the possible combinations of relations of production nor the forms in which their conditions of existence are provided can be reduced to an effect of relations between 'labourers' and 'non-labourers'. It follows that to concentrate on *those* relations must be to obscure crucial theoretical problems facing Marxist political analysis.

Conclusion

This short book is an attempt to explain some of the consequences of work in process. It cannot pretend to completeness or finality. Three definite areas for new work emerge from it. The first relates to the order of discourse - the importance in theoretical work of separating questions of the order of connection of concepts from questions of the order of connection of the social relations specified by concepts. The creation of non-rationalist forms of discursive order and non-empiricist forms of analysis of conditions of existence and effectivity are the primary problems engendered by this theoretical condition. An important caution should be offered here: this position on the order of discourse must not itself become a legislative criterion, a substitute for epistemology. The second area relates to the mode in which problems for analysis are generated in Marxist discourses. The political conditions of the appearance of questions and the status of questions as effects of certain types of political position and calculation require theorisation and critical analysis. The third area of work relates to the formation of concepts of definite social formations. It is only at this level that the concepts of relations of production, of classes, etc., acquire political pertinence which justifies their formation in discourse. For such concepts to be formed, politically conditioned questions are both a necessary and a problematic point of departure. These questions cannot simply be taken as they are given in political debate, they require critical theoretical evaluation. These three areas of work converge on the necessity of forming concepts of definite social formations, concepts which start from questions posed in the arena of political calculation and struggle.

We know that many readers, perhaps sympathetic to our theoretical aims, will respond with disappointment to these remarks. They may think that these remarks merely repeat the promises given in the Conclusion to *PCMP*,

promises of a politically relevant analysis which will in fact
never be fulfilled. We imagine others, less well intentioned
towards these pages, who will dismiss them as a 'formalist'
exercise in meta-theory. To these possible responses we can
offer here only a further promise and a challenge.

To begin with the challenge. Marxism is in no sense in a
state where it can dispense with what is often derided as
'meta-theory'. Despite its apparent intellectual vigour and
its current popularity among sections of the Western
intelligentsia, Marxist theory is riven by problems and
divisions such that it is in danger of falling into utter incoherence and methodological immobility. The current deabtes
(however lively they may appear), on the nature of the state
and the political level, on the nature and role of the 'middle
strata', on productive and unproductive labour in the definition of the working class, and on the theory of value, all
reveal fundamental ambiguities and difficulties in the basic
concepts of Marxist theory. These are not the errors of third-
rate epigones but symptoms of problems in the concepts of
Capital and other basic works of Marxist theory. We would
go so far as to say that these debates, in their very
incoherence and inconclusiveness, signal the failure of
Marxist theory to analyse modern Western capitalism. A
radical change in concepts and problems is necessary if we
are to be able to deal with the social relations and the
current political problems that confront us. A radical change
in the basic political outlook of many Marxist theorists is
also necessary if these problems are to become possible and
pertinent ones for them. For example, we would argue that
no one who believes that the present economic crisis offers
the prospect of a revolutionary situation, or who imagines
socialist policies can be implemented without, or as an
alternative to, adjustment to the conditions of international
capitalist competition, can comprehend the political tasks
facing British socialism today.

To conclude with our promise. In a co-operative work soon
to be published, we and our co-authors have attempted the
critique of *Capital* we consider necessary for the Marxist
analysis of capitalism today. The reflections offered here are
intended to clear the ground for that text. If these pages and

the pages to follow are a radical departure from previous Marxist positions, it is because we feel that this departure is politically and theoretically necessary. It is for our readers to judge their value.

Notes

1. Examples of the charges of 'formalism' and 'idealism' are to be found in the reviews of John Taylor and the late Maurice Dobb respectively.

Talal Asad and Harold Wolpe's review was not available to us when this text was written. Whilst accepting the existence of many of the inconsistencies they note, we would differ from them on their sources and significances. Rather than reply point by point to a review which lacks a clear opposed or alternative position, we feel the present text should make our position on their criticisms sufficiently accessible.

2. See Hindess (1977) and S. P. Savage, *The Sociological Theories of Talcott Parsons: Modes of Critique and Analysis of Discourse* (forthcoming) esp. chap. 1.

3. A classic example of such a sophisticated empiricism is represented by the work of Rudolf Carnap; for a discussion see the Appendix to Hindess (1973).

4. For a discussion of Weber's epistemology which emphasises this point see Hirst (1976a) chap. 3.

5. Hindess and Savage, 'Parsons and the Three Systems of Action', in H. Martins (ed.), *Parsons Revisited* (London: Macmillan, forthcoming).

6. See Hindess (1977) chap. 7.

7. Available in English in *Theoretical Practice*, 1, 2 and 6, and *Economy and Society*, vol. V, no. 3.

8. See Hirst (1976b,c).

9. See *Theoretical Practice*, 7/8; Hirst (1972).

10. Glucksmann (1972); Poulantzas (1973); Rancière (1974) (the latest of a series of critical texts).

11. See Bettelheim (1975, 1976).

12. See Badiou (1967).

13. Obviously, our change of position does affect the analysis we gave of the AMP in the sense that we have rejected the articulated combination structure which formed a significant part of that critique. However, we would continue to argue that the concept of tax/rent does not provide a viable basis for a concept of relations of production and that the functionalist hydro-agriculture thesis is an indefensible one.

14. This point was made by Roland Anrup. It caused us to begin radically to re-think our position on the dominance of the relations of production.

15. For the concept of *phénoméno-technique*, a concept of Gaston Bachelard, see Lecourt (1975) pt 1, esp. pp. 76-8, and Gaukroger (1976) for a valuable recent discussion of Bachelard which considers this concept.

16. On transference and its problems see Freud's papers 'The Dynamics of Transference' and 'Observations on Transference Love', *Standard Edition*, vol. XII.

17. This last section is taken from a draft of a chapter of a co-operative work called *Marx's Capital and Capitalism Today*, to be published in the near future.

18. In the case of the relations of production based on the legal status of slavery, the slave is separated from all the means of production including his own labour power, that is, he receives his own subsistence only because he is a necessary element in the process of production. However, persons of 'slave' status may 'rent' their own labour power; cf. *PCMP*, chap. 3.

19. We shall here distinguish between three concepts:

(i) *the division of social labour*, that is, the division of the production of society into distinct branches producing different specialised categories of product;

(ii) the *social division of labour*, that is, the division of economic positions between classes of agents coincident on the distribution of the means of production;

(iii) *the technical division of labour*, the division of functions necessary to the operation of the productive forces under conditions imposed by definite production relations.

The concepts of SDL/TDL and the relation between them will be further developed below.

References

Althusser, Louis, *For Marx*. London: Allen Lane, 1969.

Althusser, Louis and Balibar, Etienne, *Reading Capital*. London: New Left Books, 1970.

Assad, Talal and Wolpe, Harold, 'Review of *PCMP*', *Economy and Society* vol. V, no. 4 (1976).

Badiou, Alain, 'Le (Re)Commencement du materialisme dialectique', *Critique*, vol. XXIII, no. 240 (1967).

Balibar, Etienne, 'Self-Criticism', *Theoretical Practice*, 7/8 (Jan. 1973) pp.56-72.

Bettelheim, Charles, *The Transition to Socialist Economy*. Hassocks: Harvester Press, 1975.

Bettelheim, Charles, *Economic Calculation and Forms of Property*. London: Routlege & Kegan Paul, 1976.

Cutler, Antony, 'Letter to Etienne Balibar' and 'Response', *Theoretical Practice* 7/8 (Jan. 1973) pp. 51-5, 73-85.

Dobb, Maurice, 'Review of *PCMP*', *History* (Jan. 1976).

Freud, Sigmund, *Standard Edition*, vol. XII. London: Hogarth Press, 1958.

Gaukroger, Stephen, 'Bachelard and the Problem of Epistemological Analysis', *Studies in the History and Philosophy of Science*, no. 3 pp. 189-244 (1976).

Glucksmann, André, 'A Ventriloquist Structuralism', *New Left Review*, 72 (Mar.-Apr. 1972).

Hindess, Barry, *The Use of Official Statistics in Sociology*. London: Macmillan, 1973.

Hindess, Barry, *Philosophy and Methodology in the Social Sciences*. Brighton: Harvester Press, 1977.

Hindess, Barry and Hirst, Paul, *Pre-Capitalist Modes of Production*. London: Routledge & Kegan Paul, 1975.

Hirst, Paul, 'A Critique of Rancière's and Althusser's Theories of Ideology'. Unpublished mimeo, 1972.

Hirst, Paul, *Social Evolution and Sociological Categories*. London: Allen & Unwin. 1976*a*.

Hirst, Paul, 'Problems and Advances in the Theory of Ideology'. Cambridge University Communist Party pamphlet, 1976*b*.

Hirst, Paul, 'Althusser and the Theory of Ideology', *Economy and Society*, vol. V, no. 4 (1976*c*).

Lecourt, Dominique, *Marxism and Epistemology*. London: New Left Books, 1975.

Lenin, Vladimir Illich, *The Development of Capitalism in Russia* (1899), in *Collected Works*, vol. III. Moscow: Progress Publishers.

Lenin, Vladimir Illich, 'Pages from a Diary', 'On Co-operation', 'Our Revolution' and 'Better Fewer But Better' (all 1923), in *Collected Works,* vol. XXXIII. Moscows Progress Publishers, 1966.

Marx, Karl, '1857 Introduction' and '1859 Preface' to *A Contribution to the Critique of Political Economy.* London: Lawrence & Wishart, 1971.

Marx, Karl, *Critique of the Gotha Programme* (1875), in *Selected Works,* 1 vol. London: Lawrence & Wishart, 1968.

Marx, Karl, *Capital,* vol. III, (1894). Moscow: Foreign Languages Publishing House, 1962.

Poulantzas, Nicos, *Political Power and Social Classes.* London: NLB 1973.

Rancière, Jacques, 'The Concept of "Critique" and the "Critique of Political Economy" ', *Theoretical Practice,* 1 (Jan. 1971) pp. 35-52; 2 (Apr. 1971) pp. 30-49; 6 (May 1972) pp. 31-49. The final part was published separately in *Economy and Society,* vol. V, no. 3 (1976).

Rancière, Jacques, *La lecon d'Althusser.* Paris: Gallimard 1974.

Taylor, John, 'Review of *PCMP*', *Critique of Anthropology,* vol. I, no. 4/5 (1975) pp. 127-55; vol. II, no. 6 (1976) pp. 56-69.

Index